# Programs for At-Risk Students

**Essential Tools for Educators**

# The Program Evaluation Guides for Schools

*Richard M. Jaeger, Series Editor*

**Evaluating School Programs: An Educator's Guide**
  *James R. Sanders*

**Special Education Programs: A Guide to Evaluation**
  *Ada L. Vallecorsa, Laurie U. deBettencourt, Elizabeth Garriss*

**Counseling Programs: A Guide to Evaluation**
  *L. DiAnne Borders, Sandra M. Drury*

**Reading and Language Arts Programs: A Guide to Evaluation**
  *Mary W. Olson, Samuel D. Miller*

**Programs for At-Risk Students: A Guide to Evaluation**
  *Rita G. O'Sullivan, Cheryl V. Tennant*

**Mathematics Programs: A Guide to Evaluation**
  *George W. Bright, A. Edward Uprichard, Janice H. Jetton*

Rita G. O'Sullivan
Cheryl V. Tennant

# Programs for At-Risk Students

## A Guide to Evaluation

The Program Evaluation Guides for Schools
Series Editor: Richard M. Jaeger

CORWIN PRESS, INC.
A Sage Publications Company
Newbury Park, California 91320

For information address:

Corwin Press, Inc.
A Sage Publications Company
2455 Teller Road
Newbury Park, California 91320

SAGE Publications Ltd.
6 Bonhill Street
London EC2A 4PU
United Kingdom

SAGE Publications India Pvt. Ltd.
M-32 Market
Greater Kailash I
New Delhi 110 048 India

Printed in the United States of America

**Library of Congress Cataloging-in-Publication Data**
O'Sullivan, Rita G.
    Programs for at-risk students: a guide to evaluation / Rita G. O'Sullivan, Cheryl V. Tennant.
        p.  cm.  — (Essential tools for educators)
    Includes bibliographical references and index.
    ISBN 0-8039-6043-3
    1. School improvement programs—United States—Evaluation.
2. Dropouts—United States.  I. Tennant, Cheryl V.  II. Title.
III. Series.
LB2822.82.O88  1993
371.2'913—dc20                                        92-39717

The paper in this book meets the specifications for permanence of the American National Standards Institute and the National Association of State Textbook Administrators.

93  94  95  96  10  9  8  7  6  5  4  3  2  1

Corwin Press Production Editor:  Tara S. Mead

# Contents

# Series Editor's Preface

Essential Tools for Educators: The Program Evaluation Guides for Schools is a series grounded in the premise that regular evaluation of school programs can be of enormous help to school professionals—provided *they* are the ones who plan the evaluations, conduct the evaluations, and use the evaluations to guide their school improvement activities. Evaluation is a powerful tool for documenting school needs, identifying strengths and weaknesses in school programs, and discovering how to improve almost every aspect of school life. Program evaluation need not be complex or inordinately time-consuming. Simple principles and strategies are described in the initial volume of this series, *Evaluating School Programs: An Educator's Guide.* Then, specific techniques and approaches are illustrated in the program-focused guides that complete the series. Using these principles and tech- niques, teachers, principals, and other school professionals *can* plan, conduct, and interpret the findings of powerful evaluations of their curricula; of their instructional programs in mathematics, reading, language arts, and special education; of their programs for "at-risk" students; and of their counseling and personnel development programs. The principles to be learned from this series can be applied even more broadly to the evaluation of school disciplinary programs, student assessment programs, community relations programs, and other programmatic elements that are central to the successful functioning of a school.

Extensive technical training is *not* prerequisite to planning and conducting sound evaluations of school programs. Sound evaluation *does* require a desire to improve one's school, willingness to work collegially, careful attention to detail, and basic knowledge of how school program evaluations should be carried out. The ETE series provides school professionals with the last of these elements—the essential tools they need to plan and conduct effective evaluations of their school programs.

*Evaluating School Programs: An Educator's Guide* is the foundation volume in this series. It contains a clear, concise exposition of the objectives, principles, and core issues that undergird solid evaluations of school programs. By reading this guide, teachers, principals, and their colleagues will learn how to (a) determine the feasibility of conducting a school program evaluation, (b) focus a school program evaluation, (c) structure and design a school program evaluation, (d) conduct a school program evaluation, (e) interpret the results of a school program evaluation, (f) report and make use of the results of a school program evaluation, and (g) ensure that a school program evaluation is conducted ethically, damages no one, and enriches all who are associated with the program being evaluated.

Once these basic elements of a school evaluation are well understood, readers will be ready to proceed to the guide in this series that focuses on the subject area of the program to be evaluated. Each program-specific guide provides specific instruction on the evaluation of school programs in a single subject area, and each follows a consistent pattern of organization. Following an introduction that provides an overview and rationale for program evaluation in its subject area, each program-specific guide contains a sequence of vignettes (chapters) that illustrate, in detail, evaluation of a focused aspect of a school program. Collectively, these vignettes illustrate how evaluations of school programs are planned, structured, staffed, conducted, interpreted, and used. The vignettes cover a wide range of practical evaluative issues; illustrate the selection, development, and use of a large number of evaluation strategies and instruments; and show how the results of evaluation can be used to strengthen school programs. Resources at the end of each program-specific guide contain a set of research-based standards and indicators of school program quality, a road map to the use of these standards in evaluating the effectiveness and efficiency of a school program, and an annotated bibliography of selected references on program evaluation in the subject area of the guide.

Evaluations can help school professionals make their school the best it can be and, in the process, substantially increase their own educational effectiveness. In the hands of thoughtful, well-trained school professionals, evaluation can be a transformative catalyst that improves schools and all who work and learn in them. The ETE series will help you become one of those distinctive school professionals who can make school program evaluations work well. Knowing that your investment in this knowledge will pay rich dividends for years to come, I wish you every success.

RICHARD M. JAEGER
*University of North Carolina,*
*Greensboro*

# About the Authors

**Rita G. O'Sullivan** is Associate Professor of Educational Research Methodology at the University of North Carolina at Greensboro, where, for the past 7 years, she has taught graduate courses in educational program evaluation, measurement, research, and statistics. She received her B.A. in anthropology from the University of California at Berkeley, her M.A. in educational administration from California Polytechnic State University at San Louis Obispo, and her Ed.D. in educational leadership with a specialization in curriculum and instruction from Auburn University. Her primary research interests center on the methodological aspects of program evaluation. She has designed and conducted the final evaluation of a 3-year Teenage Family Life Education Program for the Ministry of Health Education and Social Welfare of the government of St. Kitts-Nevis; served as co-principal investigator of a project funded by RJR Nabisco to design a modular evaluation of the Close Up Foundation Programs in civics education; and served as evaluator for a 3-year project supported by the Fund for the Improvement of Post-Secondary Education, to increase and enhance the educational research awareness of faculty at the Historically Black Campuses of the University of North Carolina. Currently, she is investigating issues concerning the evaluation of program for at-risk populations, including dropout prevention programs, programs successful with diverse populations, and teen pregnancy prevention programs. A related research interest focuses on measurement as it influences classroom practice, because measurement poses a major problem in evaluating programs for at-risk groups. She is currently working on a project to develop and promote the use of performance assessments in conjunction with a National Science Foundation science curriculum project and the Southeast Regional Vision for Education laboratory sponsored by the U.S. Department of Education.

**Cheryl V. Tennant** (Ed.D.) is a statistical consultant and instructor at the University of North Carolina at Greensboro (UNCG). She earned her B.S. in education at the University of Tulsa, her M.Ed. in counseling, and her Ed.D. in counselor education and statistics at UNCG. She is a certified school counselor, has served as project coordinator and coauthor of the project manual for a USOE drug education program, has worked with a diverse population of clients in a mental health clinic, and has developed and conducted workshops for parents, school personnel, and professional counselors. Her research has focused on childhood issues with emphasis on the developmental aspects of decisions concerning victims' reporting of childhood sexual abuse. In addition to elementary school counseling and secondary school teaching, her prior employment includes teaching educational research at Wake Forest University and the University of North Carolina at Greensboro.

# Introduction

Conservatively estimated, one in four students who enter high school will not finish. The student dropout rate is obviously a national problem. Recognizing this problem, the president of the United States in the 1990 "State of the Union Address" identified raising the high school graduation rate to 90% by the year 2000 as an educational priority for the nation. To increase the high school graduation rate, many dropout prevention programs have been and are being implemented across the nation. The Education Commission of the States' 1987 national survey of dropout initiatives (Isenhart & Bechard, 1987) identified 190 dropout prevention program models, most of which were not in existence prior to 1983.

While the number of dropout prevention programs is growing, so too are the types of programs under the dropout prevention umbrella. Early interventions are gaining prominence in some states. Georgia, for example, has developed and implemented kindergarten through third-grade programs designed to be developmentally appropriate for students who enter school with limited academic skills. North Carolina is introducing preschool grades into the regular school prevention program in an effort to enhance academic success among students considered by the state to be at risk of academic failure.

With the number and type of dropout prevention programs growing, the need to determine the effectiveness of these programs increases. As school districts and individual schools select among dropout prevention models, their choices should be guided by information made available through sound evaluations. Once programs are begun, people working with them should be able to evaluate the programs' effectiveness for the purpose of program improvement.

## Purpose of This Guide

The purpose of this guide is to assist school personnel with the evaluation of programs designed for students at risk of academic failure.

1

With program improvement as the primary goal, evaluation procedures described in this guide are appropriate for many situations. Examples follow:

- Teachers working in an after-school tutorial program want to know whether a before-school tutorial program would serve more students.
- A middle school principal who introduced a special group guidance program for truant students wants to know how well the program is working and whether or not the students' attendance has improved.
- An elementary school staff that has just promoted its first group of students from a 2-year program for developmentally delayed kindergartners wants parents', students', and teachers' suggestions for strengthening the program.
- Secondary-level teachers assigned to a committee examining discipline procedures in a high school want to know if the in-school suspension program is decreasing the number of days students are suspended from school and decreasing the number of classroom behavior problems.
- An elementary remedial reading program director wants to know whether or not and how parents are being involved in the districtwide program.
- Middle school staff who have completely restructured their program to be more responsive to the learning styles of unsuccessful students want to know the staff's priorities for additional training.
- The staff at a newly created alternative high school want to know what criteria should be used for admitting students at risk of dropping out to the program.

In each of these situations, program personnel could use the information desired to improve practices or make effective, program-enhancing decisions. Evaluation provides a systematic way of collecting desired information.

## When to Use This Guide

Evaluation results can be used for many important purposes; a few are listed below:

    to assess need,
    to document how well a program is working,
    to determine how participants view a program,
    to demonstrate the usefulness of a particular approach,
    to examine how a particular program component is working,
    to allocate resources, or
    to provide information for setting policy.

This guide is intended to aid school personnel in designing and conducting sound evaluations to effect these purposes.

## Assumptions About Program Evaluation

**Evaluation for Program Improvement**

The most important reason to evaluate programs is to improve them. Programs are continually refined based on informal and formal evaluation. For example, a team of elementary school teachers recognizes that, in their classrooms, disruptive students are not completing their assignments and are demanding too much of the teachers' time. The teachers decide to start responding to this disruptive behavior by recognizing students who are modeling the correct behaviors in the classroom rather than directly chastising the offending students. During the next team meeting, they might decide, based on their experiences, that the program is working for everyone except two children and change their plan accordingly. This is an example of informal evaluation.

More formal assessments are needed periodically, however, to take a careful and systematic reading of a program's operation from a consistent perspective. In the example above, the team might record the number of disruptive incidents occurring during the 9 weeks prior to implementation of the positive approach and compare that with the number of such incidents occurring during the 9 weeks after the program's implementation. They could examine any differences in students' behavior they found during the two time periods, see whether the results they found matched their informal impressions, and decide how they should respond to students' disruptive behaviors in the future. Evaluation encourages program staff to reflect on a program's operation and consider areas for improvement.

The uneasiness associated with the thought of evaluation often stems from concern that outsiders, ill-equipped to evaluate a program, will misjudge it. This evaluation guide was written for school personnel. It is designed to equip teachers, principals, and other school professionals to design, conduct, and benefit from evaluation of their own school programs. Effective evaluation of schools and school programs does not require the involvement of outsiders. Teachers and other school personnel, those who know their school programs best, can use evaluative tools to make their schools better. This guide was designed to help them learn how.

## At-Risk Students and Those Who Work With Them

This guide is intended to be useful to school personnel working with school- and community-based programs serving at-risk students in preschool grades through high school. These programs include dropout prevention efforts for students who have already reached school-leaving age as well as programs for students who are academically at risk of school failure.

**Defining
*At Risk***
The term *at risk* is not meant to be another negative label associated with students struggling against failure and trying to succeed in school. Rather, the term is borrowed from the medical field, where identification of characteristics common to people who have succumbed to illness allows doctors to prescribe preventive measures. People with immediate family members who are diabetic are at risk of developing diabetes; people with high cholesterol are considered at high risk for heart disease. Based on knowledge about groups with particular ailments, doctors can identify predisposing characteristics that place individuals in high risk groups. Often, more than one predisposing factor increases the degree of risk. Obviously, the degree of risk is situational as well. A student who is 16 years old and legally entitled to leave school is in a category of greater risk for dropping out of school than a younger student. An honors students who is sent to in-school suspension once in his or her academic career is not in the same risk category as a kindergarten child arriving at school with serious language development delays or a high school student who cannot read. The term *at-risk students* is used to describe children who have not completed high school and who are considered to be at risk of academic failure.

Programs for at-risk students therefore describe special efforts by schools or other agencies to help students who are believed to be "at risk" of dropping out prior to high school graduation. These programs may begin with preschool students (e.g., Head Start), or they may work with students who have already dropped out (e.g., General Education Diploma—GED—programs operated by 2-year colleges). These programs share common approaches that emphasize similar strategies known to work well with at-risk students. Even though program intents may be different (e.g., increased school attendance, improved achievement, reduced number of students repeating the same grade), the common ground shared by these programs makes this guide relevant to their evaluation.

**How to Use This Guide**

This guide is intended to be used in concert with *Evaluating School Programs: An Educator's Guide* (Sanders, 1992), in the Essential Tools for Educators series, which is a general guide to the evaluation of school programs. The *Educator's Guide,* like this volume, is designed for use by school personnel. The *Educator's Guide* contains important information common to all evaluations that should be understood before evaluating any program. The *Educator's Guide* includes information on how to focus an evaluation, collect needed information, organize and analyze that information, and report the conclusions reached and insights gained. It also suggests ways to conduct and manage evaluations.

**Read the
General
Evaluation Guide**    This guide for evaluating programs for at-risk students is a companion to the *Educator's Guide*; it provides specific examples of how school personnel might evaluate various components of programs designed for at-risk students. This guide assumes that readers understand the information contained in the *Educator's Guide*. Familiarity with the *Educator's Guide* will provide school-based evaluators with a substantive overview of program evaluation that will enable them to organize the following evaluation activities:

> selecting members for an evaluation team,
> specifying the purpose of the evaluation and its audience,
> identifying program stakeholders,
> generating evaluation questions,
> developing an evaluation plan,
> gathering information,
> summarizing the information gathered, and
> interpreting and reporting evaluation findings.

It is strongly recommended that all school staff interested in evaluating a program for at-risk students read the *Educator's Guide* before using this guide.

**How Examples
Are Used**    This guide illustrates general evaluation approaches through examples of programs designed for at-risk students. Although the program examples were fabricated, they are based on strategies currently used in schools throughout the United States. Six programs for at-risk students are presented; each of the six programs has a unique evaluation purpose.

The evaluation situations were constructed to use previously identified standards and indicators of program quality common to successful interventions with at-risk students. These standards and indicators of quality emerged from an extensive nationwide search of programs that work with at-risk students.

This guide is not a cookbook with explicit directions on how to evaluate a particular program; rather, it illustrates how to apply general evaluation principles in six specific contexts. School personnel using this guide must apply the information provided and mold it to their particular evaluation situation. They must determine the extent to which a particular approach presented is relevant to their program evaluation needs.

**How This Guide Is Organized**

Within the context of programs for at-risk students, this guide contains suggestions for focusing an evaluation, steps to follow in the design and implementation of an evaluation, examples of how an evaluation team might evaluate a particular program component, a reference section for further reading (Resource A), a resource with a list of standards and indicators of high quality programs (including recommended evaluation methods for each indicator; see Resource B), and a reference list of evaluation reports and other sources used to identify the standards and indicators (Resource C).

**Standards and Indicators of Program Quality**

The standards and indicators in Resource B identify characteristics of high quality programs for at-risk students. *Standard* is a broader term than *indicator* and often a standard contains more than one indicator. Standards express, in general terms, characteristics of high quality programs; indicators describe more specific aspects of high quality programs. For example, Standard 3 states: "Program staff employ multiple strategies to motivate students in the program." To explain to program personnel how they might achieve this standard of quality practice, there are six indicators describing effective strategies for motivating students that are characteristic of high quality programs for at-risk students.

Standards and indicators were identified through an extensive review of the research and evaluation literature describing programs for at-risk students around the nation. The programs that were reviewed also provided convincing evidence of program effectiveness. If a program satisfied every standard and indicator, it most likely would be exemplary.

The purpose of an evaluation will determine which program aspects an evaluation team will select to evaluate. Because the standards and indicators in the appended resource are important to program quality, evaluations will often consider the important program aspects covered by the standards and indicators. School personnel generally will not use all of the standards and indicators to evaluate their programs.

This guide is *not* an introduction to the field of educational program evaluation. *Evaluating School Programs: An Educator's Guide* (Sanders, 1992), in this series, is such a guide, and members of an evaluation team should be familiar with its content. *Educational Evaluation: Alternative Approaches and Practical Guidelines* (Worthen & Sanders, 1987) is an excellent source of additional information about educational program evaluation.

Finally, the standards and indicators of program quality in Resource B that are used as examples throughout this guide might cause concern because they define components of quality programs but do not necessarily include desired program outcomes. Nowhere in this guide will program evaluation teams consider assessing changes in dropout rates or achievement test scores. These outcome measures and others are important to programs for at-risk students but are not used in the vignettes that form the body of this guide because it is erroneous to assume, and very difficult to show, that an increased graduation rate, for example, was directly due to a particular program and not to a change in school district attendance policy or a change in a state's graduation requirements. The reverse situation, where a program is very good but fails to show changes in these same outcome indicators, also could occur. The standards of quality practice that appear in Resource B identify characteristics common to effective programs for at-risk students. Determining how your program compares with the standards and making appropriate modifications should result in program improvement.

## Vignettes and How They Are Organized

Each of the six vignettes created for this guide contains

a brief description of a program setting and an evaluation focus,

a discussion of alternative evaluation strategies available to evaluation team members,

a description of how information was collected using the selected strategy,

an analysis and a summary of the information collected, and

an interpretation of how evaluation results might be used.

Each of the vignettes focuses on a different strategy for gathering information to answer evaluation questions. The strategies were selected because they represent some of the more commonly used evaluative approaches. In each vignette, one strategy is emphasized to provide the reader with detailed information for use in future applications. Multiple approaches and information sources typically are preferred, however.

The six vignettes presented address the following situations and approaches:

- Assessing students' needs using focus groups
- Identifying students for program participation and comparison groups using existing documentation
- Determining whether or not a program improves students' attitudes toward school using existing attitude scales
- Strengthening individualized instruction using an observation checklist
- Verifying, using a written questionnaire, that school staff support the program
- Establishing the level of parents' involvement in the program using interviews

References with suggestions for further reading are contained in each vignette. These references are summarized in Resource A at the end of this guide.

# 1

## Vignette One

# Assessing Students' Needs Using Focus Groups

**Focus**

**Evaluation Setting**  The Midfall County school system is located in a rural community and consists of six elementary schools (kindergarten through Grade 5), one middle school (Grades 6 through 8), and one high school (Grades 9 through 12) with an annual total enrollment of approximately 2,600 students. The middle school's leadership team (2 school administrators and 12 teachers) recently developed a 4-year plan to restructure their school so that more students at risk of academic failure would succeed. They proposed to use teams of five teachers (one each from the major academic subjects areas) to identify students' needs, to investigate alternative strategies for meeting those needs, to develop action plans for implementing change, and then to begin enacting the plans and changing the school's instructional program. These middle school teams of teachers would gradually expand their activities over the 4-year period.

In preparation for evaluating the students' needs at the middle school, the leadership team consulted *Evaluating School Programs: An Educator's Guide* (Sanders, 1992). One of the teachers on the leadership team found a needs assessment book that was very helpful: J. McKillip, Need Analysis: Tools for the Human Services and Education (1987, Newbury Park, CA: Sage). The book emphasized that need analysis provided essential information that could serve as a basis for the design of school programs and that it also allowed school personnel to establish a starting point from which to evaluate change. Needs assessment is one of the indicators of quality programs for at-risk students identified in Resource B:

*Indicator 8.1:* The program is designed based on the needs of the group being served.

## Assessing the Needs of Middle School Students

The middle school leadership team was ready to assess the needs of at-risk students at their school. They decided to meet with the entire faculty at the school to reach consensus about what it meant for their students to be at risk of academic failure. During the meeting, teachers identified low standardized achievement test scores, previous retentions in grade level, low subject grades, poor attendance, and problematic behavior as indicators that students were at risk of academic failure. Once they agreed on a definition, teachers determined which of the 600 students at the school were most at risk; however, not everyone agreed on the relative importance of the identified indicators.

The leadership team decided to find out more about the students in their school from available documentation. They discovered that

half of the students at the school had scored below the 35th percentile on the California Achievement Test Total Battery;

15 students were repeating the same grade;

one third of the students received warnings about their academic progress for the first 6 weeks of the semester;

the school's attendance rate during the first six weeks of the semester was below 85%; and

during the first 6 weeks of the semester, 10 students had been sent to the principal's office for disciplinary reasons, but no students had been suspended from school.

## What Was Already Known About Students

The leadership team met again with the school's faculty to report their findings. From the information gathered, low achievement surfaced as a high priority problem. Standardized achievement test scores indicated that approximately 15% of the 600 students were achieving below their expected level; half of the students should score at or below the 50th percentile, not below the 35th percentile. The 6-week progress reports warned that one third of the students in the school were experiencing some difficulty in their classes. The 85% attendance rate might be contributing to the low grades assigned to one third of the students.

Behavior problems did not appear to be a serious area for concern, but the team decided to review behavior information again at the end of the semester. Given that repeating a grade indicates previous academic failure, the team decided that the 15 students repeating the same grade this year needed special assistance. They requested that 15 teachers volunteer to be special advisers to students who were retained in grade.

The available information about students' achievement, behavior, and attendance helped the teachers better understand the needs of at-risk students attending their school, but they decided that they still had an incomplete picture of the situation. The teachers wanted to know what their students thought they needed to improve their academic success.

**Assessment Strategy Options**

**Deciding Among Alternative Approaches**

To collect information about students' perceptions of their needs, the middle school leadership team considered an attitude inventory about school climate, a written survey, individual interviews, and focus groups. The team decided that the school climate inventory was too indirect; they might find out about school climate but would not necessarily have the answers to their questions about students' needs. Further, the predetermined categories in the inventory that asked students if they strongly agreed, agreed, disagreed, or strongly disagreed with selected statements were too narrow. The teachers did not necessarily want students responding about their degree of agreement but instead wanted students to tell them what they thought.

The leadership team then considered using a written survey. A questionnaire could be designed to ask the questions the team wanted answered and would afford students the opportunity to respond directly to questions about their perceived needs. In addition, a representative sample of the students could respond to a written questionnaire in a reasonably short period of time and the method would not cost too much money. The leadership team was not sure that it knew the exact questions it needed to ask and was worried about the writing requirement of the questionnaire approach to gathering information. Many of the students they wanted to hear from lacked the skills necessary to respond to a written questionnaire. Among at-risk students who had the skills to respond, there also might be an aversion to writing down what they thought, fearing it might be used against them.

Individual interviews with students could avoid the problems identified with written questionnaires in this situation, but interviewing is very costly. It would be difficult to find the time, money, and interviewers to interview enough students so that the team could be confident that they had secured a representative sample of students' needs.

One of the team members thought that guided group discussions, called *focus groups,* would be suited to their purpose of identifying what students thought they needed to improve their academic success. The team members found a helpful resource on the use of focus groups in a local college library: D. L. Morgan *Focus Groups as Qualitative Research* (1988, Newbury Park, CA: Sage).

**Information Collection: Strategy and Instrumentation**

**Why Focus Groups Were Selected**

Focus groups are somewhat similar to group interviews. They can be used when group interaction is necessary to obtain information relevant to the evaluation question(s). Unlike group interviews in which participants respond only to a leader's questions, focus groups allow discussion among the participants and thereby provide additional information. The middle school team thought that students might more readily contribute their ideas during a discussion among their peers than they would if they were expected to respond only to an interviewer's questions. The discussion would also allow students to weigh the relative importance of the needs identified in the focus group.

**How to Use the Focus Group Approach**

The middle school's leadership team spent their planning period for the next week working on questions and a format for the focus group. They met again with the faculty to review their plans for the focus groups to make sure that the information they proposed to gather was appropriate to their purpose. The team decided that they would use the regularly scheduled 20-minute adviser-advisee period during the morning to conduct the focus groups. These classes were selected because they were limited to 15 students each and students were assigned to these classes randomly by grade level; therefore students with varying achievement levels were mixed together. The team could have decided to randomly select classes for participation in the focus groups but decided against it. They thought that asking each of the 40 adviser-advisee classes to participate would send a positive message to the student body that the team wanted to hear from everyone. In addition, to be fairly confident of selecting a representative sample, the team would have needed to meet with a large proportion of the 40 classes.

The middle school leadership team members decided to work in pairs, with one person leading a focus group and the other person taking notes. Five sets of focus group leaders planned to spend eight consecutive mornings conducting the focus groups. The focus group leaders pilot tested the focus group protocol developed by the evaluation team with ninth-grade students from the high school and fifth-grade students from an elementary school to make sure that the language of the questions was clear and that they could complete the protocol in the available time period. Once modifications of the protocol had been

Introduction:

We have come here today to talk to you about what we might do at school to help you do better in school. We are interested in what each of you thinks might make this a better place for you to learn and also what you as a group consider to be your most important areas of need. We're going to spend the next 20 minutes talking about this topic. Mr./Ms. X will write down what you say so that we can share it with the rest of the school. However, s/he will not write down your names, so that your comments will be anonymous outside this room. We'll give you a chance at the end of class to listen to what we've written down so that you can make sure that it is what you want people to know.

1a. What one thing could teachers do to help you succeed better at school?
    *Probe:* Why did you select that?
    (Go around the room write down what students say)
1b. Is there anything else that teachers could do that should be listed here?
1c. Look at the list. Not including your suggestions, which of the items listed is the most important?
    *Probe:* Why did you select that one?
    (Go around the room write down what students say)
2a. What one thing could you do that would help you succeed better at school?
    *Probe:* Why did you select that?
    (Go around the room write down what students say)
2b. Is there anything else that you could do that should be listed here?
2c. Look at the second list. Not including your suggestions, which of the items listed is the most important?
    *Probe:* Why did you select that one?
    (Go around the room write down what students say)
3. Can you think of anything else that might be done at school to help you succeed?
    *Probe:* Why would this help you succeed?
    (Go around the room write down what students say)

Thank you for helping us out. We'll let you know what students in the whole school thought in a few weeks, when we've finished meeting with everyone.

**Figure 1.1.** Focus Group Protocol for Assessing Students' Needs

made as a result of the pilot test, the focus group leaders were ready to begin their activities. Figure 1.1 contains the modified focus group protocol.

## Analysis and Summary of Data

**How Information Was Summarized**    At the end of each class, students reviewed their responses to the focus group questions listed in the priority sequence they determined. Middle school leadership team members organized field notes from their focus group experiences each day after school was dismissed. They consulted a book about writing up qualitative research results to help them learn how to summarize their findings: H. F. Wolcott, *Writing Up Qualitative Research* (1990, Newbury Park, CA: Sage). For each of the three questions asked, the middle school team selected the three most frequently identified areas for change. This meant that there were 120 suggestions (40 focus groups × 3) in response to the "what could teachers do" questions, 120 suggestions (40 focus groups × 3) in response to the "what could you do" question, and 120 suggestions (40 focus groups × 3) in response to the "what could be done at school" question. Members of the middle school leadership team developed a coding system for organizing the responses. First, they examined all of the responses by question and developed tentative categories. The categories were designed not to overlap so that no response could be entered into two categories. Next, they agreed on definitions for each of the categories. With these definitions, two people independently coded the responses to the questions into the various categories. They compared their classifications of the responses and revised the coding system as needed. Categories containing less than 5% of the responses and more than 25% of the responses were carefully examined to see if they should be redefined.

**Reporting What Was Found**

The middle school leadership team summarized the information collected from the focus groups. Their results are shown in Table 1.1. Students in the focus groups most commonly said that teachers needed to change their communication skills. Of the 40 focus groups, 22 listed as one of their top three priorities that teachers needed to change their ability to communicate expectations to students. Half of the focus groups identified "listening to students" as an important area for teacher change, and 18 of the focus groups said that they "needed teachers to take more time for explaining assignments."

The focus groups identified the most important areas for student change as "following directions" (23%), "listening to teachers" (21%), "doing homework" (18%), "not playing in class" (15%), "studying harder" (13%), "not talking back to teachers" (8%), and "getting help when confused" (5%). Areas in the school that students suggested for improvement were "tutors to help with work" (27%), "fewer classes" (23%), and "more time to go outside" (21%).

**Interpretation Including Pitfalls/Concerns/Cautions**

**Presenting the Findings**

The middle school leadership team shared their summary of the focus group information with the rest of the faculty at the next meeting. They cautioned the faculty that the information they collected was still preliminary but stated that they thought they had a clearer idea of some of the areas students considered important to change. They pointed out to the faculty that the test scores, grades, and attendance information they had collected earlier indicated which outcomes

**TABLE 1.1**  Students' Suggestions for Improvement Identified During the Focus Groups

| Areas of Improvement | Number of Focus Groups Listing Among Top Three Priorities | (%) |
|---|---|---|
| Areas teachers need to change: | | |
| better explanation of expectations | 22 | (18) |
| listening to students better | 20 | (17) |
| more time to explain assignments | 18 | (15) |
| less homework | 15 | (13) |
| less talking/more activities | 13 | (11) |
| more interesting work | 12 | (10) |
| more extra credit | 8 | (7) |
| more time in class to help with work | 7 | (6) |
| more enjoyable classes | 5 | (4) |
| Areas individual students need to change: | | |
| following directions | 28 | (23) |
| listening to what the teacher says | 25 | (21) |
| doing homework | 22 | (18) |
| less playing in class | 18 | (15) |
| studying harder | 16 | (13) |
| no talking back to the teacher | 10 | (8) |
| getting help when confused | 6 | (5) |
| Other areas identified for change: | | |
| tutors to help with work | 32 | (27) |
| fewer classes | 27 | (23) |
| more time to go outside | 25 | (21) |
| time to meet with friends | 14 | (12) |
| someone to talk to about problems | 12 | (10) |
| being able to chew gum | 10 | (8) |

of the instructional program needed improvement, whereas the results of the focus groups identified strategies that students thought needed improvement.

**Pitfalls/ Concerns/ Cautions**    The faculty consensus was that the focus group information was important and allowed them to view the school's needs from the students' perspectives. The leadership team cautioned that these perspectives were that of the adviser/advisee classes and not those of individual students. When focus groups were selected as a data collection method for the evaluation, rather than individual student assessments (e.g., written surveys or face-to-face interviews), the information collected represented group opinions. Some students might have been reluctant to share their views in the group. Opinion leaders in the class might have influenced other students' comments. Therefore the information presented had to be interpreted at the classroom level. In addition, the information did not separate at-risk students from more successful students.

**Applying the Results**

The faculty decided as a group to use the students' suggestions from the focus group surveys to improve their classroom instruction. They asked the leadership team to build on the results of the focus groups by designing an interview protocol to be used with selected at-risk students to see if the results represented those students' views. The faculty also wanted more information about differences in responses by grade level. They asked the middle school leadership team members to further analyze the focus group information in Table 1.1 to show students' responses for each grade level.

**Evaluation Principles**

This vignette illustrated a number of important principles of good evaluation practice. These principles include the following:

1. Consulting with different groups who are interested in the program (stakeholders) allows multiple perspectives for identifying important evaluation issues. The leadership team did not make decisions about the evaluation without first meeting with the principal and other teachers in the school to tap their thoughts about at-risk students who were attending their school. It is possible that the leadership team members might have missed issues important to other members of the faculty had they not talked with them.

2. Using available documentation saves time and valuable resources. The leadership team used the school's records from the previous year. They reviewed standardized tests scores, promotion statistics, attendance records, and disciplinary actions to determine the most important problem areas. Had the leadership team decided to reassess achievement using a new standardized test, very little new information would be expected. A new achievement assessment also would have taken time and resources to administer, score, and interpret.

3. Selecting an assessment strategy from among alternatives promotes an evaluation that is responsive to specific problems and evaluation purposes. Focus groups were not the only assessment strategy considered for the evaluation. By comparing the advantages of focus groups with written questionnaires and individual interviews, the leadership team could weigh the relative advantages of the different assessment approaches in light of their evaluation needs.

4. Focus groups require careful planning before they are conducted. The leadership team systematically developed the focus group questions and format. The teachers at the school reviewed the questions and

plans for the focus group. The leadership team members pilot tested the focus group with similar groups of students before conducting the focus groups in their school.

# 2 Vignette Two

## Identifying Students for Program Participation and Comparison Groups Using Existing Documentation

**Focus**

**A Program to Ease the Transition Into High School**

Longview High School and Middle School recently began a new dropout prevention program for at-risk students. The purpose of the program was to assist at-risk students with the transition from eighth grade at the middle school to ninth grade at the high school. The high school's principal supported the program, because she knew that disproportionate numbers of students dropped out of the high school during their first semester. A survey of the high school's dropouts for the past 5 years indicated that the students who had dropped out during that first semester of ninth grade did so because they were not doing well academically and felt no connection to the school.

The program was designed in two phases. The first phase would take place during summer school: 30 at-risk eighth-grade students would be invited to participate in an alternative summer school program that would promote their academic achievement and enhance their high school survival skills. These students would be selected from among students who needed to successfully complete summer school

19

as a requirement for promotion to ninth grade. Two teachers and 10 peer tutors (high school students) would be selected to work with the program participants during the summer program. The second phase of the program would start at the beginning of the participants' ninth-grade year. Students from the summer program would be enrolled in a special study-skills class at the high school. The peer tutors from the summer program would assist with this class and were expected to meet with participants at least once a week, outside of the study-skills class.

**Planning the Evaluation**

The principal met with the program staff in February to discuss their progress in planning the program that was scheduled to begin that summer. She also worked with them on developing an evaluation plan that would assess the program's effectiveness. Constructing an evaluation plan at the beginning of the program enabled the periodic collection of important information by which to gauge students' progress. The principal knew that evaluation should be an integrated part of program planning.

The program staff wanted information that would allow them to determine whether or not the program increased students' academic achievement, improved their attendance, reduced the number of their discipline referrals, and prevented students from dropping out of the high school. They also wanted to know whether students' attitudes about school improved and whether participation in the program contributed to a student's sense of belonging at the high school.

**The Importance of a Comparison Group**

The principal knew that determining program effectiveness was an important standard of program quality for at-risk programs. Resource B includes the following:

> *Standard 8:* Adequate provision is made for assessing the effectiveness of the program.

Further, the principal knew that assessing the effectiveness of this program could best be accomplished by comparing participants with a comparison group. The program staff needed to consider who the program would serve and with whom participants might be compared to assess the program's probable impact. A comparison group allows contrasts to be made supposing no program had occurred. For example, if 3 of the 30 students in the program left school in the first semester of their ninth grade, the program staff would have no way of knowing whether this was a higher or lower dropout rate than would be expected without the program. Program staff might use the previous year's dropout statistics, but they would then have to find a way to determine whether this year's group of students was comparable to last year's.

Because the program only had funds to serve 30 students and there were more than 60 eighth-grade students eligible for summer school, the principal suggested that they compare the 30 program participants with 30 regular summer school students. The program staff had to decide how they would identify students for the program and for the comparison group.

**Assessment Strategy Options**

The program staff could have designed a form for the eighth-grade teachers to complete, requesting information about each student's grades, standardized test scores, attendance, behavior, attitudes about school, and level of involvement with school. The teachers' responses to these questions could then have been used to identify which of the students should be invited into the program. The program staff also might have administered an attitude questionnaire to the students to identify students who did not express positive feelings about the school's program. If a special form or questionnaire were created to identify students for participation in the program, however, those surveyed might respond by trying to anticipate the program staff's intent.

An interview with the students about their experiences in and attitudes toward school might be used instead of a written questionnaire. The face-to-face interview would allow follow-up questions about the students' views to be posed and might therefore provide a fuller description of the relevance of the program to the students. During the interview, the students also might be asked whether they were interested in participating in the program.

**The Advantages of Using Existing Documentation**

The program staff then considered the use of existing documentation to identify students for the program and for the comparison group. Whenever possible, existing documentation should be consulted and used. Occasionally, people mistakenly believe that new data collection forms are necessarily better than existing ones. If the regular record keeping system in the school included sources of information about students' achievement, attendance, behavior, or attitudes toward school, then a form to duplicate that information would not be necessary. Duplication of information should not be confused with using multiple sources to verify the accuracy of information collected. In this situation, using multiple sources of information to identify students for participation in the program would increase the likelihood of selecting appropriate candidates.

Another advantage of using existing documentation is that it is an "unobtrusive measure," the use of which does not disrupt the usual flow of school events. Use of existing documentation is not problem free, however. A potential problem with using existing documentation is that it may be incomplete and/or inaccurate. One advantage that a school-based team has over an outside evaluation team is that they are usually aware of documentation problems. If poor record keeping is a problem, it should not be ignored. There is no point in basing decisions on inaccurate information.

**Additional Information Sources to Consult**

For more information about using existing documentation and unobtrusive measures, see N. S. Metfessel and W. B. Michael (1967), "A Paradigm Involving Multiple Criterion Measures for the Evaluation of the Effectiveness of School Programs," *Educational and Psychological Measurement, 27,* 931-943, and E. J. Webb, D. T. Campbell, R. D. Schwartz, and L. Sechrest (1966), *Unobtrusive Measures: Non Reactive Research in the Social Sciences* (Chicago: Rand McNally).

After weighing the alternatives, the program team decided that the documentation available at the school would be appropriate for identifying students to participate in the program as well as those to serve as a comparison group. They decided to use standardized eighth-grade achievement test scores, grades, and attendance information available on report cards for the third-quarter grading period and at-risk referral forms filled out by teachers at the end of every academic year.

## Information Collection: Strategy and Instrumentation

**Identifying the Documentation Needed**

Toward the end of eighth grade, after standardized achievement test scores are returned to the school districts, school counselors are required by the state's Department of Education to compile a list of all students scoring below the 25th percentile compared with a national norm group on a standardized test. Students scoring below the 25th percentile must take a minimum skills competency test. If they fail to score above 70 on the minimum skills test, they must successfully complete summer school to enter ninth grade. With 365 students enrolled in Longview Middle School's eighth-grade class, the program staff used the school counselor's list to identify students for the program. Of the 365 eighth-grade students, 100 scored below the 25th percentile of the norm-referenced standardized achievement test. Ten of those students were receiving special education services and were deleted from the list.

For the remaining 90 students, report card information for the third 9-week grading period was collected, noting number of courses failed and number of absences since the beginning of the school year. In addition, the counselor had on file at-risk referral forms filled out by the students' seventh-grade teachers at the end of the previous school year. The number of teachers who completed an at-risk referral

**TABLE 2.1**    Summary Information Sheet for Identifying At-Risk Students

| Student | Percentile Test Score | Absences | Number Fs | Number of Teacher Referrals |
|---------|----------------------|----------|-----------|----------------------------|
| 1 | 15 | 20 | 3 | 4 |
| 2 | 24 | 15 | 2 | 1 |
| 3 | 9 | 5 | 3 | 2 |
| 4 | 11 | 35 | 4 | 3 |
| 5 | 17 | 22 | 1 | 2 |
| 6 | 19 | 3 | 2 | 1 |
| 7 | 10 | 40 | 5 | 5 |
| 8 | 7 | 15 | 3 | 4 |
| 9 | 23 | 2 | 0 | 2 |
| 10 | 12 | 11 | 2 | 1 |

form at the end of seventh grade for each of the 90 students was tallied. The summary information sheet used to compile all of the available documentation for the students is shown for 10 of the 90 students in Table 2.1.

**How Information Was Gathered**

The information was relatively easy to collect, because the categories used to identify the students were selected, in part, due to availability of information. The school counselors had already developed an alphabetized list of students scoring below the 25th percentile on the eighth-grade standardized test and had listed students' total-battery percentile scores with students' names. Duplicate report cards for all students were kept in the school's central office and were alphabetized by grade level. Therefore collecting report card information did not require going to students' individual record folders. Finally, the at-risk referral forms teachers had filled out were kept on file in the guidance office and were alphabetized and sorted by grade level and year. Project staff were able to compile the information about the 90 students in a few days.

## Analysis and Summary of Data

Looking at the list of 90 students and the information they had gathered, the program staff decided they needed a systematic way of determining each student's degree of risk. It appeared that Student 4, who scored in the 11th percentile, was absent 35 days, failed four courses, and was identified as at-risk by three teachers, might be at greater risk of dropping out of school than Student 9, who scored in the 23rd percentile, was absent 2 days, failed no courses, and was identified as at risk by two teachers. They decided to create an at-risk rating scale based on a weighted point system.

**Developing an At-Risk Rating**

The program staff had studied reports of previous dropout prevention programs (see Resource C for relevant references) and had found examples of how other programs had used at-risk rating scales to identify students. They discussed possible rating systems with the schools' teachers, counselors, and administrators. They reasoned that there were different levels of risk within the indicators they had identified and that students with multiple high level risk factors would be more likely to drop out of school. They expected that weighting the scale would increase the likelihood of distinguishing among students' degree of risk.

The program staff decided to assign the following weights to their at-risk rating scale:

- Standardized Achievement Test Scores:
    15th-24th percentile = 1 point
    less than 15th percentile = 2 points
- Absences:
    0-9 absences = 0
    10-19 absences = 1 point
    20-29 absences = 2 points
    30-39 absences = 3 points
    40-49 absences = 4 points
- Number of Fs:
    No Fs = 0
    1-2 Fs = 1 point
    3-4 Fs = 2 points
    5-6 Fs = 3 points
- Number of Teacher Recommendations:
    no recommendations = 0
    1-2 recommendations = 1 point
    3-4 recommendations = 2 points
    5-6 recommendations = 3 points

Although the decisions about creating categories and assigning points within categories was arbitrary, the program staff thought that this approach was consistent with their program needs. For each student, the collected information shown in Table 2.1 was transformed into an at-risk rating scale value. For example, Student 1 received 1 point for his test score at the 15th percentile, 2 points for his 20 absences, 2 points for the three failing grades, and 2 points for the four teachers' recommendations. His at-risk rating therefore was 7. Table 2.2 shows the at-risk ratings for the 10 students listed in Table 2.1.

**TABLE 2.2**  At-Risk Rating Scale Values

| Student | Percentile Test Score | Absences | Number Fs | Number of Teacher Referrals | At-Risk Rating |
|---------|-----------------------|----------|-----------|------------------------------|----------------|
| 1 | 15 = 1 | 20 = 2 | 3 = 2 | 4 = 2 | 7 |
| 2 | 24 = 1 | 15 = 1 | 2 = 1 | 1 = 1 | 4 |
| 3 | 9 = 2 | 5 = 0 | 3 = 2 | 2 = 1 | 5 |
| 4 | 11 = 2 | 35 = 3 | 4 = 2 | 3 = 2 | 9 |
| 5 | 17 = 1 | 22 = 2 | 1 = 1 | 2 = 1 | 5 |
| 6 | 19 = 1 | 3 = 0 | 2 = 1 | 1 = 1 | 3 |
| 7 | 10 = 2 | 40 = 4 | 5 = 3 | 5 = 3 | 12 |
| 8 | 7 = 2 | 15 = 1 | 3 = 2 | 4 = 2 | 7 |
| 9 | 23 = 1 | 2 = 0 | 0 = 0 | 2 = 1 | 2 |
| 10 | 12 = 2 | 11 = 1 | 2 = 1 | 1 = 1 | 5 |

From the At-Risk Rating column in Table 2.2, Student 7, with an at-risk rating of 12 points, would be considered to be at greatest risk of dropping out; and Student 9, with 2 points, would be considered to be the least at risk of dropping out.

### Creating Matched Pairs to Identify Based on the At-Risk Rating

Assuming the program staff completed an at-risk rating for all 90 students, each student could be ranked according to the rating assigned. If students were placed in pairs according to their at-risk ratings, one of each pair could be randomly assigned to the program with his or her partner assigned to the comparison group. For example, if only the 10 students in Table 2.2 were paired by their at-risk rating, the following matching might occur:

Student 7 (12 points) and    Student 4 (9 points)
Student 1 (7 points) and    Student 8 (7 points)
Student 3 (5 points) and    Student 5 (5 points)
Student 10 (5 points) and    Student 2 (4 points)
Student 6 (3 points) and    Student 9 (2 points)

### Random Assignment to Program and Comparison Groups

By flipping a coin 5 times (heads, the student in the left column is invited into the program; tails, the student on the right), Student 7, Student 8, Student 5, Student 3, Student 2, and Student 9 might be selected into the program. This would leave Student 4, Student 1, Student 3, Student 2, and Student 6 in the comparison group. If, for some reason, a student did not participate in the program or left the program, the partner that student was paired with would be dropped from the comparison group.

**Interpretation Including Pitfalls/Concerns/Cautions**

Employing existing documentation to develop an at-risk rating system to select students for a program and comparison group can be a useful strategy. The decision to use existing information rather than to conduct interviews or to administer questionnaires to assess students' attitudes toward school saved time and money. The availability of multiple measures by which to select students also enhanced the use of available documentation.

**Combining Existing Documentation With Other Approaches**

For those cases in which the existing documentation is limited and/or suspect, augmenting the available information by collecting additional data would be appropriate. Often, existing documentation will allow initial screening of students for selection into a program. With a reduced number of students, additional data collection procedures become more feasible. For example, once the list had been reduced from 365 to 90, it would have been reasonable to ask the school's administrators to review the 90 names and make recommendations about students' inclusion in the program. These ratings then could be incorporated into the at-risk rating scale.

Of course, the at-risk rating scale is not a perfect system for identifying students for a program. Students who might benefit greatly from the program might not be selected for participation. An important indicator of risk might be overlooked. Program staff need to look critically at the information available for each student before they develop an identification process. Certainly, examination of available information is always a good starting point.

**Applying the Results**

The program staff used the at-risk rating scale to invite students to participate in the summer school program. The school guidance counselor was given the list of the 45 students who had been selected from each pair to participate in the program. Students were listed in order from highest to lowest on the at-risk rating scale. The program staff asked the guidance counselor to begin calling students and their parents at the top of the list and to stop when she had 30 acceptances.

**Evaluation Principles**

This vignette illustrated a number of important principles of good evaluation practice. These principles include the following:

1. Integrating the evaluation design with program planning permits systematic collection of important information by which to judge a program's effectiveness. The principal met with program staff to review how plans for the program were progressing as well as to assist them with the evaluation plan. If they had waited until the comple-

tion of the program to decide on the information they needed for the evaluation, the data easily might have been impossible to collect.

2. Contrasts about program effectiveness are possible when a comparison group is identified. The program intended to ease the transition from middle school to high school for at-risk students. At the end of the first year of the program, perhaps five students might have left school. Without a comparison group, it would be very difficult to determine if five dropouts indicated an effective or ineffective program. The presence of a comparison group allowed the program staff to compare similar groups of students and contrast the dropout rates with and without the program.

3. Multiple indicators often identify a characteristic more accurately than a single measure. The program staff decided to combine standardized achievement test scores, number of absences, number of subjects failed, and teacher referrals so as to identify students who were at risk of dropping out of school. The program staff could have selected just one of these indicators, but that probably would have led to some at-risk students not being identified for participation in the program.

4. Finding examples of how professionals implementing similar programs conducted their evaluations can provide the evaluation team with ideas and procedures to use. The program staff studied reports of previous dropout prevention programs and found examples of how they used at-risk rating scales. They probably saved time and resources by consulting these evaluation reports.

5. Using unobtrusive measures limits disruption of the regular school program and eliminates certain response bias. Existing documentation is considered an unobtrusive measure. No new data collection efforts were needed to develop the at-risk rating scale. In addition, by using indirect indicators of the students' risk of dropping out, the at-risk rating was not influenced by a students' desire to participate in this program.

# 3

## Vignette Three

# Determining Whether or Not the Program Improves Students' Attitudes Toward School Using Existing Attitude Scales

**Focus**

According to the most recent statewide study to estimate school dropout rates, Curry School System, a large metropolitan school district, had the highest number and percentage of students leaving school before high school graduation. The Curry Board of Education, alarmed by the survey results, created a task force to investigate alternative strategies for retaining students in school. After 6 months of study, the task force members returned to the school board with a report that emphasized the importance of early intervention to keep students in school.

**Teachers as Tutors in Elementary Grades**

After reviewing early intervention models for dropout prevention used in other school districts, Dr. George Keely, assistant superintendent for curriculum, recommended that the school board fund a pilot program in six of the elementary schools (kindergarten through fifth grade). The purpose of the program was to improve students' academic achievement and attitudes toward school. The program used flexible scheduling and classroom aides so that teachers could provide individual tutoring for students who were behind academically. Teachers worked in teams by grade level, planning instruction and identifying students' tutoring needs. Teachers spoke weekly with the parents of the at-risk students in their teams because of the importance teachers placed on involving parents in the instructional program.

**Identifying Evaluation Criteria**

An advisory committee (the principal and one teacher from each of the six elementary schools) met monthly with Dr. Keely to discuss the program's progress and problems. During the summer prior to program implementation, the advisory committee asked how they should judge program effectiveness. The group's consensus was that they could use examples of students' work, grades, and standardized achievement test scores to assess growth in students' achievement, but they were not as comfortable in measuring changes in students' attitudes toward school. Promoting positive attitudes toward school is one of the indicators of quality programs for at-risk students identified in Resource B:

> *Indicator 3.4:* Program staff promote students' positive attitudes toward school.

**Assessment Strategy Options**

**Considering Alternative Approaches**

To assess how well the tutoring program promoted students' positive attitudes toward school, the advisory committee might have chosen to interview teachers and students or to have them complete written questionnaires. Interview information could have been collected by directly asking teachers what strategies they used to promote positive attitudes toward school among students and asking students whether or not they thought the teachers were doing a good job improving their attitudes about school. Responses to those types of questions very likely would have been less than honest, however, due to the pressure to provide socially acceptable answers. Teachers were aware that they were expected to improve students' attitudes toward school and would have been foolish to admit doing otherwise. It also is possible that teachers were engaged in activities they thought would improve students' attitudes but that, in fact, were not effective. Finding the time necessary to interview teachers and students would be a problem too, because interviews require extensive interviewer time.

**Developing an Attitude Scale**

Developing a written attitude scale to distribute to teachers and students would solve the cost problem associated with interviews. It would not, however, solve the issue of receiving socially desirable answers to direct survey questions. In addition, developing and using a valid and reliable scale to assess students attitudes is a serious undertaking (see *Evaluating School Programs: An Educator's Guide,* Sanders, 1992, pp. 26-28). In many settings therefore, the development of an attitude scale is not feasible because the cost exceeds the available funds.

**Selecting Among Existing Attitude Scales**

Fortunately, sources of well-constructed attitude scales exist. There are reference books that describe published and unpublished attitude scales (among other assessment instruments) and often include information about the validity and reliability of these scales. Such sources might provide an existing scale that was appropriate for the evaluation's purpose or, at least, a scale suitable for adaptation.

One source of commercially available attitude scales is J. V. Mitchell, *Tests in Print III* (1983, Lincoln: University of Nebraska, Buros Institute of Mental Measurements). Another source to consult about measuring attitudes is M. E. Henerson, L. L. Morris, and C. T. Fitz-Gibbon, *How to Measure Attitudes* (1987, Newbury Park, CA: Sage).

**Information Collection: Strategy and Instrumentation**

**Identifying the Most Appropriate Instrument**

The advisory committee decided that the most efficient and feasible information collection strategy was to use or modify an existing attitude scale to measure students' attitudes toward school. They consulted test directories and discovered four instruments that appeared to meet their needs. They obtained copies of these attitude scales and reviewed them according to the six criteria suggested in *How to Measure Attitudes* (Henerson, Morris, & Fitz-Gibbon, 1987). For each of the four instruments, the advisory team members answered the following questions:

- Does the instrument assess what it claims to measure?
- Does the instrument fit our evaluation purposes?
- Does the instrument provide consistent responses to questions?
- Is the measurement appropriate for the intended group?
- Are there any problems that might result from using the measure?
- Is it practical to use the instrument?

One of the four attitude measures, *Attitude Toward School K-12* (Los Angeles: Instructional Objectives Exchange, 1972), appeared best suited to their evaluation. It appeared to assess students' attitudes toward school in a way that was consistent with the evaluation purposes.

The estimated reliability of the instrument was acceptable, indicating reasonably consistent responses to questions. Different forms of the instrument had been developed appropriate to the grade levels to be assessed. Pilot testing of the instruments with students in nonparticipating elementary schools affirmed that students found the wording of the scale understandable. Finally, permission to use and copy the instruments was granted by the publisher, thereby greatly reducing the cost of using the instrument.

**Selecting Who Should Respond to the Attitude Scale**

Due to the ease with which the attitude scale could be administered, the advisory committee decided to assess the entire population of students in the six schools rather than selecting a sample of students for the evaluation. The advisory committee agreed that all of the teachers in the six schools would benefit from knowing each student's attitude toward school. This assessment would establish a baseline measurement indicating where the students began and help identify areas of concern for new program development. Subsequent attitude assessments could be compared with previous ones to indicate change brought about by the program.

**Training Teachers to Administer the Attitude Scale**

Teachers administered the attitude scale to approximately 3,500 students in the six schools. Prior to administering the attitude scale to students, participating teachers attended an after-school workshop where they reviewed the two forms of the instrument (one for kindergarten through Grade 2 and one for Grades 3 through 5), discussed the purposes of the assessments and how the results would be used, and practiced administering the instruments. This training was intended to promote uniform administration of the attitude scales.

Students were told that there were no right or wrong answers to the questions but that the school staff wanted to know their feelings about the statements on the attitude scale. Students also were assured of anonymity, because their names would never be put on the response sheets. Class and teacher information were coded onto the instrument by students at the beginning of the data collection session. Teachers read questions to students. The school counselors subsequently administered the attitude scale to the students who had been absent.

Figure 3.1 contains the attitude scale that was administered to 1,750 third through fifth graders at the six elementary schools.

### Analysis and Summary of Data

Each of the surveys was summarized by class with the number of students responding to a particular question noted. The summary sheet for one class of responses appears in Figure 3.2.

Directions: For each statement, indicate the extent to which you agree or disagree by circling the letter of your choice.

|     |                                    |
| --- | ---------------------------------- |
| SA  | if you strongly agree              |
| A   | if you agree                       |
| D   | if you disagree                    |
| SD  | if you strongly disagree           |

| | | | | |
|---|---|---|---|---|
| 1. Each morning I look forward to coming to school. | SA | A | D | SD |
| 2. I hate having to do homework. | SA | A | D | SD |
| 3. Most of my teachers give assignments that are just busywork. | SA | A | D | SD |
| 4. Most of my teachers really like their subjects. | SA | A | D | SD |
| 5. School is a good place for making friends. | SA | A | D | SD |
| 6. Most of the decisions in my classes are made by the teachers. | SA | A | D | SD |
| 7. Most of my teachers give me some idea of what will be on their tests. | SA | A | D | SD |
| 8. School is just a place to keep kids off the street. | SA | A | D | SD |
| 9. I try to do good work in my classes because you never know when the information will be useful. | SA | A | D | SD |
| 10. Many of my teachers have "pets." | SA | A | D | SD |
| 11. Most of my teachers often waste too much time explaining things. | SA | A | D | SD |
| 12. Occasionally I have discovered things on my own that were related to some of my school subjects. | SA | A | D | SD |

**Figure 3.1.** School Sentiment Index
SOURCE: This attitude scale was taken from Instructional Objectives Exchange. (1972). *Attitude Toward School: Grades K-12*. Los Angeles: Author. Permission to use and copy has been granted by the publisher.

## Ways to Summarize the Information

The class summary sheets were then put together by grade for each school. In addition to reporting the numbers of students responding to each statement in each of the four categories, percentages were calculated. Percentages made the information easier to understand and made it possible to compare groups that differed in size.

## Coding the Information

At the school district level, the assistant superintendent wanted to compare schools in the program. The advisory committee members used a point system to code the responses. For each of the 12 items contained in the scale, the following point system was used: 4 = strongly agree, 3 = agree, 2 = disagree, and 1 = strongly disagree. Items 2, 3, 6, 8, 10, and 11 in Table 3.1 marked with an asterisk are reversed items with the point score reversed. The points are reversed because strongly agreeing to a response would indicate a negative attitude toward school. For example, a student strongly agreeing with statement 2, "I hate having to do homework," would probably strongly disagree with a positive rewording of that statement. The points assigned therefore are reversed to keep the scale consistent. Thus the maximum

| Statements | Strongly Agree | Agree | Disagree | Strongly Disagree |
|---|---|---|---|---|
| School: BRYAN ELEMENTARY | | | Class: JONES | |
| Total Enrollment: 25 | | | Grade: 5 | |
| 1. Each morning I look forward to coming to school. | 7 | 5 | 5 | 8 |
| 2. I hate having to do homework. | 10 | 11 | 3 | 1 |
| 3. Most of my teachers give assignments that are just busywork. | 5 | 7 | 8 | 5 |
| 4. Most of my teachers really like their subjects. | 6 | 11 | 6 | 2 |
| 5. School is a good place for making friends. | 19 | 4 | 1 | 1 |
| 6. Most of the decisions in my classes are made by the teachers. | 10 | 5 | 7 | 3 |
| 7. Most of my teachers give me some idea of what will be on their tests. | 6 | 8 | 4 | 7 |
| 8. School is just a place to keep kids off the street. | 2 | 5 | 12 | 6 |
| 9. I try to do good work in my classes because you never know when the information will be useful. | 1 | 4 | 18 | 2 |
| 10. Many of my teachers have "pets." | 5 | 6 | 8 | 6 |
| 11. Most of my teachers often waste too much time explaining things. | 9 | 8 | 5 | 3 |
| 12. Occasionally I have discovered things on my own that were related to some of my school subjects. | 2 | 3 | 10 | 5 |

**Figure 3.2.** School Sentiment Index Summary by Class

possible score for any individual would be 48 and the minimum score would be 12. The higher the score, the more positive the student's attitude toward school.

**Comparing Two Schools**

A comparison of students' responses at two schools is presented in Table 3.1 to demonstrate how the information might be summarized and used. Percentages of students in each group who selected each response choice are shown by group. From the percentages for each response, it is clear that the two school groups had almost opposite response patterns on 8 of the 12 statements, with School 1 demonstrating a less positive attitude toward school than School 2. On questions 6, 7, 9, and 12, response patterns were closer for the two groups.

Because all of the items on this modified scale assess the same general attitude, a total score was calculated for each student. Students' scores were then averaged for the two groups. The average attitude score for School 1 students was 25.9. The average score for School 2 students was 31.5.

**TABLE 3.1**  Responses to the School Sentiment Index School Comparisons

| | Percentage of Students School 1 | | | | Percentage of Students School 2 | | | |
|---|---|---|---|---|---|---|---|---|
| | SA | A | D | SD | SA | A | D | SD |
| 1. Each morning I look forward to coming to school. | 15 | 20 | 56 | 9 | 26 | 30 | 29 | 15 |
| 2. I hate having to do homework.* | 44 | 25 | 21 | 10 | 15 | 24 | 46 | 15 |
| 3. Most of my teachers give assignments that are just busywork.* | 37 | 35 | 20 | 8 | 15 | 14 | 66 | 5 |
| 4. Most of my teachers really like their subjects. | 18 | 25 | 45 | 12 | 35 | 22 | 38 | 5 |
| 5. School is a good place for making friends. | 23 | 20 | 27 | 30 | 31 | 40 | 15 | 14 |
| 6. Most of the decisions in my classes are made by the teachers.* | 42 | 30 | 18 | 10 | 24 | 48 | 16 | 12 |
| 7. Most of my teachers give me some idea of what will be on their tests. | 24 | 30 | 36 | 10 | 43 | 32 | 20 | 5 |
| 8. School is just a place to keep kids off the street.* | 62 | 28 | 7 | 3 | 10 | 27 | 33 | 30 |
| 9. I try to do good work in my classes because you never know when the information will be useful. | 3 | 12 | 46 | 39 | 6 | 15 | 55 | 24 |
| 10. Many of my teachers have "pets."* | 60 | 19 | 15 | 6 | 18 | 33 | 37 | 12 |
| 11. Most of my teachers often waste too much time explaining things.* | 14 | 48 | 28 | 10 | 11 | 29 | 42 | 18 |
| 12. Occasionally I have discovered things on my own that were related to some of my school subjects. | 18 | 47 | 20 | 15 | 44 | 22 | 30 | 4 |
| Average Total Score | | 25.9 | | | | 31.5 | | |

*Reversed items with the point score reversed.

## Interpretation Including Pitfalls/Concerns/Cautions

**Results of the Comparison Between Two Schools**

With 48 the maximum possible score and 12 the minimum possible score, an average score of 25.9 indicates that School 1 students disagreed more than they agreed with statements considered to reflect positive attitudes toward school (a score of 30 would be considered "neutral"). School 2's attitude toward school was more positive. Such results seem consistent with what is expected, because School 1 has higher proportions of at-risk students than School 2.

**Value of Norm-Group Comparisons**

Unlike some published attitude scales, the one used did not provide information about how an individual or group compared with a larger group. Although this type of norm-group comparison is not essential, it would have been interesting to see how the students' scores compared with those of other elementary school students nationally. Certainly, it will be important for the evaluation to have the students retake the attitude scale later in the school year. Administering the attitude scale again near the end of the school year would allow the advisory committee to see if there had been any improvement in students' attitude toward school.

**Cautions About the Attitude Scale Used**

The results of this evaluation must be interpreted cautiously. While the attitude scale has been validated and the reliability estimated, the results still are not conclusive. Using only the general attitude items resulted in a relatively short scale. The advisory committee might consider integrating some of the other subscales from the original attitude scale to improve the instrument's validity and reliability. Another indicator of or method for assessing students' attitudes toward school should be considered to enhance the fidelity of the findings; multiple methods would increase confidence in the results. Finally, students' attitudes toward school should be examined carefully considering expected variation by grade level. Students' responses may change over time. Fourth graders' attitudes toward school may be generally more positive than fifth graders' attitudes toward school.

**Applying the Results**

From the information gathered and summarized, the teachers decided to increase their efforts to promote positive school attitudes among students. They also thought that it would be helpful to look at the attitude scale results by classroom. Differences among the classes in students' positive attitudes would warrant further investigation. Certainly, the evaluation information confirmed for the teachers that students' attitudes toward school varied by school at the beginning of the school year. Comparisons across schools needed to be carried out carefully and evaluation determinations about program effectiveness at each school needed to be anchored to each school's context.

**Evaluation Principles**

This vignette illustrated a number of important principles of good evaluation practice. These principles include the following:

1. Using previously developed and tested measurement instruments is usually preferable to constructing them. Developing a valid and reliable scale is resource intensive. The advisory committee recognized that it would be better to amend an existing attitude instrument than expend most of their available time and resources developing an attitude measure.

2. Comparing similar instruments to see which best suits the purpose of the evaluation will result in the collection of useful information. The advisory team was able to identify four instruments that measured students' attitudes toward school. From those four, they could select the instrument that best suited their evaluation needs.

3. Establishing a baseline measure at the beginning of a program is important in making comparisons later. The advisory committee decided to measure the students' attitudes toward school at the beginning of the program, because no other measure was available to indicate where the students began. Subsequent measures of students' attitudes toward school could be compared with the baseline measure to indicate changes brought about by the program.

4. Training in the purpose and administration of measurement instruments promotes uniform assessment practices. The teachers, who were the ones asked to administer the attitude scale, received training in conducting the assessment. In this way, the advisory committee could be fairly sure that the 3,500 students completing the attitude scale would do so under similar conditions.

# 4

## Vignette Four

# Strengthening Individualized Instruction Using an Observation Checklist

**Focus**

The principal at Middletown Elementary School wanted the 15 teachers in her school to improve their ability to individualize instruction for students. Many of the 375 students attending the kindergarten through second-grade primary school were already considered academically at risk. A survey of parents who just completed registering their children for kindergarten revealed that many of the students had not gone to preschool. The preliminary kindergarten screening assessment showed that many of the students lacked the readiness skills usually related to school success. Older students in the school had difficulty meeting state promotion standards, and 10% were repeating the same grade this year.

**Learning Styles Instruction in the Primary Grades**

The principal was convinced that instruction based on each student's needs would increase students' academic success. Before the academic year began, the principal organized a workshop on learning styles instruction for the teachers. The workshop leader demonstrated how matching students' preferred learning styles with instructional practices can result in improved academic success; often, at-risk students' preferred learning styles mesh least with traditional instructional practices. Although the teachers were hesitant to change their teaching practices completely, they were willing to initiate some classroom activities that would appeal to more learning styles. The workshop leader then assisted teachers with constructing learning centers for students; these centers used instructional approaches other than paper-and-pencil learning activities. Students were to spend at least 1 hour each day using the learning centers.

## Using Learning Centers to Individualize Instruction

After the first 9 weeks of school, teachers were mixed in their reactions to the learning centers. Some teachers thought the learning centers were a great asset to instruction and wanted to expand their efforts. Other teachers voiced concern about the effectiveness of the learning centers. These teachers worried that the learning center activities lacked the flexibility to promote success for all students. The variability in students' ability made it difficult to design learning center activities appropriate for the different skill levels. While most of the teachers agreed that individualizing instruction to tap students' learning style strengths was ideal, some expressed concern that the learning center activities were not consistent with this ideal. A number of the teachers also were skeptical of the learning center approach to instruction and thought that at-risk students would benefit more from drill and practice.

## Deciding What to Evaluate

After considering the teachers' concerns, the school principal decided to evaluate the learning centers in the school. The principal, the school counselor, and three teachers volunteered to work on the evaluation team. The evaluation team met and proposed that they evaluate the learning center activities to see whether or not different learning modalities were actually used and to determine the levels of success students were experiencing with the current learning center activities. The team considered these evaluation activities important, because individualizing instruction by accommodating students' preferred learning styles is one of the indicators of quality programs for at-risk students identified in Resource B:

> *Indicator 4.2:* Lessons are planned to accommodate different learning style strengths and are not limited to paper-and-pencil activities.

### Assessment Strategy Options

The evaluation team met with the teachers to discuss possible evaluation strategies. They decided to use a peer-review process to assess the extent to which their learning center activities accommodated various learning styles. The evaluation team, supported by the teachers, chose to wait until later in the academic year to assess the impact of the learning center activities on students' achievement. The entire group agreed that they needed to examine students' success with the current learning center activities.

**Focusing the Evaluation**

The evaluation team considered surveying teachers in the school as a possible data collection strategy for assessing students' success with learning center activities. Interviews or written questionnaires could have provided information about teachers' perceptions of the learning centers and teachers' thoughts concerning learning centers' contribution to students' success. The evaluation team decided against using either survey technique, however, because the teachers had already questioned the effectiveness of the centers and further probing their concerns did not seem to be a good use of evaluation resources.

**Considering Alternative Approaches**

The evaluation team could review the teachers' lesson plans and grading books to assess the students' level of success with the learning centers. One evaluation team member observed that not all teachers maintained their lesson plans with the same amount of detail. Of the 15 teachers, 1 had elaborate notes about the learning center activities in her lesson plan book, but another of the teachers only had a brief outline. It would have been difficult to judge the learning centers from this type of secondary data. Neither would it have been possible to judge how the learning centers, as described, were actually implemented or how the centers worked with the students in the program.

**Classroom Observations**

Classroom and school observations can be a valuable source of information for program evaluation (see *Evaluating School Programs: An Educator's Guide,* Sanders, 1992, pp. 28-29). Such assessments may be the only means of answering evaluation questions pertaining to the actual classroom implementation of an instructional program. Documents indicate what was recorded, surveys reflect what people report, but observations report what the observer saw in the classroom, thereby supplying the evaluator with information that cannot be obtained through other methods of data collection.

Observations are not without problems. Validity and reliability can be an issue, because two observers assigned to a classroom to observe and take notes would not necessarily have the same understanding of what they were supposed to observe or be likely to record the same thing. Numbers of observations made and length of observations also can be problematic; the observer must be in the classroom observing typical behavior and not something out of the ordinary. These problems can introduce bias, thus misrepresenting the program.

There are certain recommended precautions that help to minimize these types of observer bias. Training of observers in observation techniques before sending them to the classroom is important. Scheduling a series of observations over an extended period of time will increase the likelihood that observers obtain a reasonably accurate picture of reality. Using an observation checklist to guide the observation and facilitate information gathering also is very helpful.

For more information about observation checklists, see A. Simon and E. G. Boyer, editors, *Mirrors of Behavior: An Anthology of Observation Instruments* (1974, Philadelphia: Research for Better Schools). For more information about classroom observations, see J. J. Gallagher, G. A. Nuthall, and R. Rosenshine, editors, *Classroom Observation* (AERA Monograph Series in Curriculum Evaluation No. 6; 1970, Chicago: Rand McNally).

## Information Collection: Strategy and Instrumentation

**Organizing the Evaluation**

After careful consideration of their options, the evaluation team chose observation checklists as the method to gather the relevant information. Members of the evaluation team met with the teachers to identify observable behaviors or events that would help them evaluate how well the learning center activities were encouraging student success. The evaluation team generated a list of possible learning center observations and circulated that list to the entire professional staff with an explanation of the evaluation. Staff were encouraged to return their comments to the evaluation team, and volunteers were requested to serve as observers for the evaluation. The school counselor agreed to work with classes on a group guidance curriculum, thereby providing volunteer teachers with released time for classroom observations.

**Constructing an Observation Checklist**

Four additional teachers volunteered and worked with the evaluation team to construct the observation checklist and the observation procedures. From the list that was circulated and the discussions that followed, teachers said that students with successful experiences at the centers would (a) know what to do at the center, (b) stay on task and talk with other students only about the learning center activity, and (c) be able to complete the center activity with limited assistance from a teacher and within the specified time period. The following events, therefore, were identified for observation: (a) student's arrival time at the learning center, (b) an indication of whether the student began to work immediately with learning center materials, (c) number of student and teacher interactions about learning center activity, (d) number of student and teacher interactions about non-learning center activity, (e) number of student's interactions with other students about learning center activity, (f) number of student's interactions with other students about non-learning center activity, (g) whether student completes the learning center activity, and (h) student's departure time from the learning center. These behaviors and events were placed in an observation checklist format, shown in Figure 4.1, to increase the ease and consistency of observer reporting. Teachers who volunteered as observers were trained to use the observation checklist using videotapes of students working at learning centers.

Arrival and departure time calculations would allow for an assessment of how much time a student spent at the learning center. More than the allotted time at the center with an uncompleted activity might indicate that the activity was too difficult for the student or that the students needed assistance staying on task. Information concerning teacher-student and student-student interactions during the learning center time might demonstrate that an activity required too much teacher supervision for students to experience successful independent learning or that a child finding an activity too easy spent his or her remaining time socializing with other children.

## Scheduling Observations

In each classroom, students participated in four 15-minute learning center activities every day. Teachers were allowed to select which of the four activities they wanted observed. Because the learning centers could not be observed continuously, the team decided to observe each classroom learning center for 60-minute periods at random times with half of the observations done during the morning hours and half done during afternoon hours. The four teachers observed learning centers in each of the 15 classrooms four times (two mornings and two afternoons) for a total of 60 observations completed by each volunteer teacher. Each of the 15 learning centers was observed 16 times.

## Analysis and Summary of Data

## Summarizing the Information

A summary of the findings for one of the learning center's 16 observation sessions follows. Table 4.1 shows the average length of time students spent at the center and average number of interactions with teachers and other students while at the learning center. In all, 32 students were observed at this learning center during a 2-month period with 3.6 average student visits per observation session. Of the students, 15 (43%) began work immediately once they arrived at the center and 22 (67%) completed the center activity. On average, students had slightly more interactions with teachers about learning center activities

Teacher: _____ Date of Visit: _____

Time: from _____ to _____

Observer: _____

**Directions:** Each time a student comes to the learning center, start a new column.

1. Note the time in the space provided at the top of the column.

2. If student begins to work immediately with learning center materials, put a hatch mark (/) in the box below the first box in the same column.

3. Every time a student and teacher interact about the learning center activity, put a dot in the box. Dots should follow this pattern:

4. Every time a student and teacher interact about non-learning center activity, put a dot in the box following the same pattern as in number 2.

5. Every time a student interacts with another student about a learning center activity, put a dot in the box following the same pattern as in number 2.

6. Every time a student interacts with another student about non-learning center activity, put a dot in the box following the same pattern as in number 2.

7. If the student completes the learning center activity, put a hatch mark (/) in the box.

8. Note the time of the student's departure from the learning center in the last box of the same column.

|                                                                        | Student 1 | Student 2 | Student 3 | Student 4 |
|------------------------------------------------------------------------|-----------|-----------|-----------|-----------|
| 1. Student's arrival time                                              |           |           |           |           |
| 2. Student begins to work                                              |           |           |           |           |
| 3. Student and teacher interact about learning center activity         |           |           |           |           |
| 4. Student and teacher interact about non-learning center activity     |           |           |           |           |
| 5. Student interacts with other students about learning center activity |           |           |           |           |
| 6. Student interacts with other students about non-learning center activity |       |           |           |           |
| 7. Student completes learning center activity                          |           |           |           |           |
| 8. Student's departure time                                            |           |           |           |           |

Use back of the sheet for any additional comments about the observation session.

**Figure 4.1.** Learning Center Observation Checklist

**TABLE 4.1**  Summary of Students' Activity at Learning Center X (*n* = 32)

| Characteristics | Number |
|---|---|
| Student's average time at the learning center (minutes) | 12 |
| Students who began work immediately | 15 |
| Average student and teacher interactions about learning center activity | 1.5 |
| Average student and teacher interactions about non-learning center activity | 1.1 |
| Average student interactions with other students about learning center activity | 0.5 |
| Average student interactions with other students about non-learning center activity | 3.0 |
| Students completing learning center activity | 22 |
| Students receiving feedback from teacher about learning center activity | 25 |

(1.5) than non-learning center activities (1.1). Students averaged 3.0 interactions with other students about non-learning center activities compared with an average of 0.5 interactions with other students about learning center activities. Of the 32 student visits to the learning centers, 25 visits included teacher-student interactions. Of the observations indicating no teacher-student interactions, 5 involved students who did not complete the learning center activities.

**Interpretation Including Pitfalls/Concerns/Cautions**

**Reporting the Information Found**

The above results suggest that the learning centers were being used. Less than half of the students (15) were able to begin work without delays, while 17 needed some assistance in this area. The reason for such delay should be investigated to determine the cause. Did these children lack understanding of what to do or were the activities too difficult? In most cases, students (22) were able to complete the learning center activity, indicating that the level of the activity was appropriate. Ten students did not complete the assignment, however, suggesting the need for further inquiry. Although this information does not directly inform a decision about the effectiveness of the learning centers in promoting students' achievement, it does indicate whether or not the centers are operating as intended.

**Cautions About the Results**

Interpretation of this assessment must be done cautiously and with the understanding that the results are suggestive and not conclusive. The evaluators cannot be certain that the results of their observations are truly representative of the classroom learning centers or the students. The times randomly selected for observation may not have been representative of all the learning center activity time.

**Possible Distractors**     Another factor that may have affected the results is the presence of an observer. Some students may have been motivated to work more diligently in the presence of an observer, while some students may have been distracted by the observer. The teachers also might have been affected by the evaluation. For example, some teachers might have devoted more time to each student at the learning centers during the observations than they do when not being observed. Another consideration relevant to the interpretation is the possibility that the checklist was too short to adequately sample the learning center activities. An evaluation cannot be more valid than the instruments used.

**Applying the Results**     Evaluation team members reviewed the results with the teachers. The teachers decided that they wanted to increase the numbers of students who completed the learning center activities. They decided to review the information collected to see if they could identify the students who had the most difficulty completing learning center activities. The teachers would talk with these children about their difficulties and report back to the group to suggest possible causes. They asked the evaluation team to schedule another set of observations later in the school year to assess any changes in the indicators.

**Evaluation Principles**     This vignette illustrated a number of important principles of good evaluation practice. These principles include the following:

1.  Validity of observations can be an issue. The evaluation team recognized potential weaknesses of the method and were careful to define the behaviors they wanted observed. They recruited four additional teachers to help them develop the observation checklist and procedures.
2.  Training observers contributes to the reliability of observation. All teachers in the program who volunteer to observe were trained to use the observation checklist using a videotape of students working at learning centers. This promotes consistency across observers.
3.  Observations should be scheduled over an extended period of time and observation times during the day should be varied. The evaluation team decided to observe each classroom learning center for 60-minute periods at random times with half of the observations done during the morning hours and half done during the afternoon. Each of the learning centers was observed 16 times.

# 5

## Vignette Five

## Verifying That School Staff Support the Program Using a Written Questionnaire

**Focus**

**A**BC Middle School is one of six middle schools in the city's school district and serves 1,100 students in sixth through eighth grades with 44 teachers on the faculty. There has been growing concern in the school district about the rising number of students who are dropping out of school. The district is interested in improving school success among children at risk of dropping out, but there are no additional funds available to support new program efforts. The superintendent of schools therefore has requested that each of the schools in the district form Student Review Committees responsible for creating positive interventions using existing resources for at-risk students in their schools.

**Middle School Teachers Show Interest in At-Risk Students**

The principal selected the school's assistant principal, three teachers, and the school counselor to serve on the Student Review Committee. One activity promoted by the Student Review Committee at ABC Middle School is the "Special Friends Program." The purpose of the program is to have each of the teachers in the school show special interest in an at-risk student. The Student Review Committee planned the program, met with teachers in groups and individually to garner support for the programs, and then coordinated assignments of students to teachers.

The Student Review Committee met at the beginning of the school year to identify students they considered to be at risk of academic failure. They determined the degree of students' risk using teachers' recommendations from the previous school year, standardized achievement test results, and attendance during the first 6 weeks of the semester. The committee circulated their initial list of at-risk students to the faculty, giving the teachers an opportunity to amend the list.

**Evaluation Purpose**

The Special Friends Program was one of four interventions the Student Review Committee was currently sponsoring for at-risk students. Because teachers were volunteering their time to participate in these programs, committee members wanted to assess the level of faculty support for the program. They wanted to know how the program was working and how it might be improved. They also wanted to find out whether the teachers thought that the program warranted their time investment or whether their time could be better spent working with one of the other three programs.

The Student Review Committee understood the necessity of faculty support for program success. Staff support for a program is one of the indicators of program quality found in Resource B:

> *Indicator 10.3:* The school program staff provides leadership and support for appropriate program practices.

### Assessment Strategy Options

**Alternative Evaluation Approaches**

The Student Review Committee decided that they wanted to hear about the Special Friends Program from individual teachers to see what proportion of them supported the program. Focus groups therefore would not be appropriate, because group discussion might influence teachers' responses. Next, the committee considered individually interviewing the teaching staff to collect the information necessary for their evaluation. Interviews would have allowed the interviewers to establish rapport with the teachers, thereby encouraging candid responses. Also, interviews would have allowed probing to clarify details, ask additional questions, and increase the accuracy of the interviewer's understanding of responses. For their purpose, however, the Student Review Committee decided that the disadvantages associated with interviews outweighed the advantages. Such disadvantages include the lack of anonymity, problems regarding scheduling, and time consumption.

Another common method for finding out the answers to program evaluation questions is to use a written questionnaire. A written questionnaire presents a collection of specific questions for people to answer. Due to the program-specific nature of written questionnaires, evaluators often must create an instrument to collect the information necessary for a particular evaluation; questionnaires successfully used elsewhere provide assistance in this task.

If they were to use written questionnaires, the Student Review Committee would further have to decide the types of questions to be asked. They read about questionnaires in *Evaluating School Programs: An Educator's Guide* (Sanders, 1992, pp. 23-25) and knew that questionnaires may contain fixed-alternative items and/or open-ended items. They preferred to mix the two types of questions so that the fixed-alternative items would allow teachers to respond easily and permit straightforward coding and analyses of the information collected about the program, while the more difficult to code and analyze open-ended items would encourage a wider range of possible responses.

**Written Questionnaires**    As it became clear that written questionnaires were the most appropriate approach available, the committee identified two sources of information about constructing, administering, coding, and analyzing questionnaire information: (a) D. Berdie and J. Anderson, *Questionnaires* (1974, Metuchen, NJ: Scarecrow), and (b) R. M. Jaeger, "Survey Methods in Educational Research" in R. M. Jaeger, editor, *Complementary Methods for Research in Education* (1988, Washington, DC: American Educational Research Association).

**Information Collection: Strategy and Instrumentation**

**Advantages of Using Written Questionnaires**    Use of a written questionnaire seemed to be the best option for collecting the information necessary for the evaluation. To evaluate the teachers' support for the Special Friends Program, the Student Review Committee needed to identify program factors that the teachers perceived as positive (successful aspects of the program) and negative (unsuccessful aspects of the program). In addition, the evaluation required information concerning the reasons teachers classified a particular aspect of the Special Friends Program as positive or negative. For example, did teachers believe the Special Friends Program was effective because students tried harder for someone who cared about their school success or because, as special friends, the teachers were able to be advocates for the students within the school?

Directions: The purpose of this questionnaire is to survey your experiences with the Special Friends Program this semester and find out how it might be improved. You are very important to the program and we thank you for your assistance in evaluating this effort.

Answer Items 1-3 by circling your response choice and then stating your reason(s) for the choice you made.

1. Do you think that you spend enough time every
   week with your special friend?                    Yes        No        Undecided

Reasons for your answer? _____

_____

_____

_____

(Use the other side of this page for additional space.)

2. Overall, do you think that the energy you devote to
   the Special Friends Program could be better spent in
   another dropout prevention effort?                Yes        No        Undecided

Reasons for your answer? _____

_____

_____

(Use the other side of this page for additional space.)

3. Generally, has the school success of your special
friend increased since the beginning of the semester?  Yes        No        Undecided

Reasons for your answer? _____

_____

_____

(Use the other side of this page for additional space.)

**Figure 5.1.** Special Friends Program: Faculty Support Questionnaire (page 1 of 4)

## Constructing Written Questionnaires

To structure their evaluation questions, members of the Student Review Committee met informally with teachers to identify the program aspects that needed investigation. From the information they gathered informally, committee members drafted a questionnaire to be distributed to all 44 teachers participating in the Special Friends Program. The questionnaire was designed with both limited-alternative and open-ended items. Twelve areas of interest about the program were identified. (See Figure 5.1 for the first page of the questionnaire containing three sample questions.)

Before distributing the questionnaire to the teachers, the team asked five teachers from one of the middle schools in the district with a similar program to complete the questionnaire and offer suggestions for its improvement. After this field test, a few changes were necessary. The questionnaire was then ready for use. Faculty were told during a

**TABLE 5.1**   Frequency and Percentage of Teachers Responding to Special Friends Program
Questionnaire, Items 1-3 (*n* = 44)

| Question | Yes (%) | No (%) |
|---|---|---|
| 1. Do you think that you spend enough time every week with your special friend? | 5 (11.4) | 39 (88.6) |
| 2. Overall, do you think that the energy you devote to the Special Friends Program could be better spent in another dropout prevention effort? | 18 (40.9) | 26 (59.1) |
| 3. Generally, has the school success of you special friend increased since the beginning of the semester? | 16 (36.4) | 28 (63.6) |

faculty meeting that they would be surveyed about the Special Friends Program in 1 week. This announcement permitted them some time to think about the program before responding to the questionnaire.

During the next faculty meeting, time was allotted for the distribution, completion, and return of the questionnaires. Of the total teaching staff, 95% (i.e., 42) were present and willing to complete the questionnaire. The remaining 2 teachers completed the questionnaire upon their return to school.

**Summary of Data**

**Responses to the Written Questionnaire**

For Items 1-3, the frequency and percentage of the teachers' responses are listed in Table 5.1. Notice that none of the teachers used the possible "undecided" alternative available on the questionnaire. Five teachers (11.4%) thought they spent enough time with their special friend, but the remaining 39 teachers did not. Teachers were more equally divided on the next two questions, with 26 (59.1%) reporting that they did not think that their effort would be better spent in another dropout prevention activity and 28 (63.3%) reporting that they had not seen an improvement in their special friends' school success.

**Results of the Written Questionnaire**

The reasons for the various responses were summarized by creating categories of responses from the individual questionnaires. This type of content analysis allowed for the grouping of similar responses to the open-ended items. Members of the Student Review Committee independently reviewed responses to each question, grouped the information, and then compared their efforts, mediating discrepancies.

With regard to the first question about sufficient time with their special friend, five teachers responded "yes." (Two said that they had the students in class daily and saw the students at least once a week

**TABLE 5.2**   Summary of Reasons Teachers Think Special Friends Have
                Increased Their School Success

*Question 3:* Generally, has the school success of your special friend increased since the beginning of the semester?

| Responses | Number |
|---|---|
| Yes responses (16 teachers): | |
| Improved attendance | 8 |
| Students wanted to do well | 5 |
| Fewer behavior problems | 3 |
| No responses (28 teachers): | |
| Students behavior problems in the classroom | 20 |
| Problem patterns already too severe | 4 |
| Lack of response to the program | 4 |

after school for tutoring. Two said that they had set up special times during their planning periods to meet with the students. One said that her special friend did not demand more time than was usually given to students having difficulty in her classroom.) Of the 39 teachers saying that they did not spend enough time with their special friends, 20 explained that they did not have their special friends in one of their classes; 15 cited students' absences; and 4 stated that their special friends were reluctant to meet with them.

The reasons given for the responses to the second question about time better spent in other dropout prevention efforts were as follows: (a) 10 of the 18 teachers responding "yes" said that they did not think their efforts were having a positive effect on their special friend, and (b) the remaining 8 teachers said that they wanted to reach more than just one of the at-risk students. Of the 26 teachers responding "no," 20 said that it was still too early to tell; the remaining 6 did not identify a reason.

**Summary of Responses to Open-Ended Question**

Reasons teachers gave for their responses to the third question about the special friend's increased school success appear in Table 5.2. Among the 16 teachers who reported that the Special Friends Program improved students' academic success, 8 identified improved attendance as the cause. Five teachers suggested that the students' desire to do well in school was a reason for increased academic success. Three teachers said they saw fewer behavior problems. For the 28 teachers who did not think that students had improved their school success, 20 observed troublesome behavior from the students; 4 said that students' problem patterns were too severe; and 4 listed the indifference of students to the program.

**Interpretation Including Pitfalls/Concerns/Cautions**

In general, the three questionnaire items depict teachers who are experiencing difficulty with the Special Friends Program. Lack of time for special friends was the most serious concern expressed among the group of 44 teachers; 39 (88.6%) reported that they did not spend enough time with their special friends because they did not regularly see these students in class. Among the five teachers who answered that they spent enough time with their special friends, only two stated that they were spending extra time with their special friends. It is unclear whether teachers understood that they were expected to spend extra time with their special friends or whether they thought that spending extra time would be of benefit to at-risk students.

**Using Evaluation Results to Improve the Program**

Twenty teachers, almost half the teaching staff, cited classroom behavior problems with special friends as a reason that the Special Friends Program did not improve students' school success. The consistency of responses suggests that this problem warrants further investigation. Recognizing the seriousness of this problem and trying to remedy it could contribute to gaining additional support from the staff for the Special Friends Program.

The questionnaire reported staff sentiment on a number of issues. The open-ended items allowed teachers to clarify why they thought certain areas of the Special Friends Program were problematic while others were not. As with any single method of collecting information, the questionnaire left much unanswered. Other methods of probing the staff's support of the program should supplement the questionnaire. For example, information from students' attendance and behavior records should be compared with the teachers' reported perceptions. Individual interviews with selected teachers could further probe the nature of the issues raised by the questionnaire.

**Applying the Results**

Based on the survey findings, a number of recommendations to improve the program were made to the faculty. First, the assigned teacher should be able to see his or her special friend daily. Second, the Student Review Committee should readjust special friend assignments in those cases where teachers report that students are reluctant to participate. Finally, members of the Students Review Committee should lead discussion among the teachers about their experiences with their special friends to clarify expectations about time investments and possible program successes.

**Evaluation Principles**

This vignette illustrated a number of important principles of good evaluation practice. These principles include the following:

1. Questionnaire designers should decided whether to use written fixed-alternative items or open-ended items (or both). The Student Review Committee preferred to mix the two types of questions to determine the teachers' overall assessment of the program and the reasons for their assessments.

2. Specifying the information to be gathered by the questionnaire is essential. After consulting informally with teachers, the Student Review Committee identified 12 areas of interest about the program. From those 12 areas, they drafted items for the questionnaire.

3. All surveys should be pilot tested before being used to make sure directions, format, and questions are clearly understood by respondents. The Student Review Committee asked five teachers from one of the middle schools to complete the questionnaire and offer suggestions for its improvement.

4. When items on a written questionnaire require thoughtful responses, adequate time should be allowed. Teachers were told about the questionnaire and its contents 1 week before its distribution. This announcement permitted them some time to think about the program before responding to the questionnaire.

5. Response rates for written questionnaires should be as high as possible. The more people who complete the questionnaire, the more confident evaluators can be that the responses represent the entire sample. By distributing the written questionnaire during a faculty meeting and allotting time for its completion, the Student Review Committee obtained a 95% response rate to their written questionnaire.

6. The content analysis of responses to open-ended items should be repeated to promote consistency of findings. Members of the Student Review Committee independently reviewed responses to each of the open-ended items, grouped the information, and then compared their efforts, mediating discrepancies.

# 6

## Vignette Six

# Establishing the Level of Parents' Involvement in the Program Using Interviews

### Focus

**Parent Involvement at the High School**

At a recent public meeting of the Littletown School Board, a representative of a local community organization protested that parents were not being involved in the instructional program at the high school and that this was particularly true for the parents of students who were not succeeding in the school system. A school board member's response indicated that school personnel were doing everything they could, but the group of parents in question was very difficult to contact and reluctant to come to school. The superintendent for the Littletown School System believed in the importance of parent involvement in the schools and therefore decided to investigate the community group's charges and report back to the board.

The superintendent instructed his assistant to gather the relevant parent involvement information on file in the various annual reports compiled by the four high schools in the system. The superintendent met with the principals to discuss the concerns about parent involvement and to explore with them ways they might assess the level of parent involvement at their schools. The four principals acknowledged some difficulty in promoting parent involvement among the parents of their at-risk students but were fairly confident that most parents received information about student progress from teachers.

Increased parent involvement was a goal the school district had set for the coming year, so the superintendent thought the issue was a timely one for investigation. He formed an evaluation team made up of the four principals, his assistant, and the dropout prevention coordinator. The superintendent also offered the evaluation team additional staff resources so they could directly survey parents.

**Evaluation Focus**
The evaluation team met and agreed to survey the degree of parent involvement in the classroom and parents' attitudes about such involvement. The evaluation therefore addressed the following indicators of quality:

> *Indicator 6.1:* Parents confer with teachers about students' progress.
> *Indicator 6.2:* Parents assist with the instructional program.

## Assessment Strategy Options

**Considering Written Questionnaires**
The evaluation team met to consider their information gathering options. There was no existing documentation on file to answer their evaluation question; neither could they locate a previously developed survey that addressed their purposes. Due to the nature of the information needed for their evaluation, the team discussed the use of a mailed questionnaire. The advantages of such an assessment device made it an attractive option. The mailed questionnaire would be relatively inexpensive; a large number of people could be surveyed with ease; no additional staff would be needed to interview parents; and people would probably answer more truthfully because their responses would be anonymous.

The disadvantages of a mailed questionnaire were discouraging to the evaluation team. The low response rate often associated with mailed surveys was problematic, because the very group the superintendent was interested in surveying would not be likely to respond to a written questionnaire. In addition, the evaluation team was interested in eliciting from parents suggestions for increasing parent involvement to meet the school district's goal for the coming year. Responses such as "I don't know" or "I'm not sure" needed to be probed. Finally, the questionnaire would not allow development of rapport with the parents. Rapport would encourage parents to respond to the survey questions. A mailed questionnaire therefore was eliminated as a possible data collection device.

**Considering Interviews**

The evaluation team then considered conducting interviews as an option for collecting information about the evaluation questions. They consulted *Evaluating School Programs: An Evaluator's Guide* (Sanders, 1992, pp. 25-26) and found that interviewing is one of the most common methods used for obtaining program evaluation information. Interviews can be structured or unstructured. The structured interview consists of fixed questions while the unstructured interview is an open situation governed by the interviewer. While based on fixed questions, the structured interview maintains the advantage of being flexible and therefore adaptable to individual situations. The interview appeared to meet the evaluation team's needs for flexibility and adaptability to allow the interviewer to restate questions in case parents did not understand the original question and/or if they did not answer the question completely.

Evaluation team members were further encouraged in that the interview, unlike self-administered questionnaires, would result in not only a high response rate but also immediate responses. The interviewer could be sure of who answered the question, and the interview procedure would be effective for gathering the information needed. The interview also appeared more appropriate than a written questionnaire for collecting information from people who would not be comfortable with paper-and-pencil tasks.

Once the evaluation team decided to use face-to-face interviews, they consulted the following books for more information: (a) R. L. Gorden, *Interviewing: Strategy, Techniques, and Tactics* (1975, Homewood, IL: Dorsey), and (b) E. G. Guba and Y. S. Lincoln, *Naturalistic Inquiry* (1985, Beverly Hills, CA: Sage).

## Information Collection: Strategy and Instrumentation

**Identifying Parents for Interviewing**

The evaluation team decided to focus their efforts on the parents of those students participating in a districtwide Afterschool Tutorial Program. The Afterschool Tutorial Program served all four high schools as a central site where students who were in danger of failing academic subjects received tutoring during the semester. Students who received unsatisfactory progress reports during the first 6 weeks of the semester had to enroll in the Afterschool Tutorial Program for the remainder of the semester. Classes were offered at various hours after school (including weekends), and transportation was provided.

Approximately 300 students were enrolled in the Afterschool Tutorial Program, and the evaluation team reasoned that the parents of the students enrolled were the population they wanted to survey. The evaluation team members wanted to contact as many parents as possible but knew realistically they only had the resources to complete

150 interviews. From the list of 300 students enrolled in the program, a team member picked one student randomly and then proceeded down the list selecting every other student until 150 students were identified. The parents of the 150 students selected would be interviewed. Evaluation team members asked the tutors in the Afterschool Tutorial Program to approach the parents about scheduling an interview time. The evaluation team was fairly confident that parents approached by their children's tutor would readily agree to an interview, thereby limiting sampling bias due to nonrespondents.

Tutors would contact the parents selected for interviews, but the interviews would be conducted using the assistance offered by the superintendent. In this way, parents would receive initial contact from someone they knew but would be interviewed by someone with whom they might be more honest about perceived shortcomings in the parent involvement component of the program.

## Defining the Scope of the Interview

The information necessary to evaluate parent involvement in the classroom included the type of contact parents had with the regular high school about their child's progress, their volunteer activity at school, the reasons parents did or did not volunteer, and their thoughts about how the school could increase parent involvement. To collect this information, the evaluation team, headed by the school counselor, wrote questions to be used in the interview. (See Figure 6.1 for the interview questions.)

## Training Interviewers

The evaluation team asked the afterschool tutors to review the interview questions for needed revisions. The evaluation team members trained 10 school district interviewers to use the interview protocol. The instrument was pilot tested during the training using parent volunteers. The following suggestions were helpful in both presenting the interview and writing the responses to interview questions:

- Respect the interviewee.
- Be genuine.
- Use language appropriate for the interviewee.
- Keep questions short and simple.
- Avoid leading questions.

The tutors contacted the selected parents to explain the purpose of the interview, ask for parent participation, let them know that the interview was not intended to take more than 15 minutes, inform them that their participation was completely voluntary, and determine convenient interview times. Interviews were scheduled at the Afterschool Tutorial Program site, and parents were offered transportation.

Interviewer:_____

Parent's Name:_____ Student's Name: _____

Scheduled Interview: _____ (date) and _____ (time)

Place of Interview: _____

Directions to Interview Site: _____

Telephone Number of Interview Site:_____

Other Telephone Number Where Parent Can Be Reached:_____

  Time interview began: _____ Time ended: _____

Directions: *When you locate the person you are to interview, say to him or her:*

Hello! My name is _____, and I am here from the Littletown School District to ask you some questions about your involvement in your son's and/or your daughter's high school program. I believe that Ms./Mr. _____, your child's tutor, contacted you about this interview. The interview should not take longer than 15 minutes of your time. You should know that your participation is voluntary and you may choose not to answer a question, or you may decide to end the interview early if you like.

The purpose of this interview is to find out how you have been involved, if at all, in the high school program. All your answers will be kept confidential and neither you nor your child will be identified by name in reporting the results of this interview.

*Ask the questions on the following page and record the responses in the space provided:*

1. Have you talked with someone at school about your child's progress
   during the last grading period?   Circle one:                    YES        NO
       If yes:  Who was that person?_____
                Who asked for the meeting?_____
                What did you talk about?_____
                _____

       If no:  Have you seen your child's report card
                for this grading period?   Circle one:      YES        NO
       Would you like to talk to someone at the high school
                about your child's progress?   Circle one:  YES        NO
2. Have you volunteered in the high school this year?   Circle one:   YES        NO
       If yes:  What did you do? _____
                Would you do it again?   Circle one:        YES        NO
       What could be done to increase the help you give at school?
       _____

       If no: What could be done to increase the help you give at school?
       _____

3. What suggestions do you have about how we can get more parents to volunteer to work in the classroom?
       Would you like to receive a summary report of all the
                interviews that were done?   Circle one:     YES        NO

Is there anything else you would like to let us know at this time? (Write comments on back of page.)

Thank you very much for your time and your help. If you have any questions or think of anything else you would like to tell us, please contact the principal or assistant principal at Littletown High School.

**Figure 6.1.** Parent Interview

Each of the 10 interviewers scheduled 15 interviews at the parents' convenience.

## Analysis and Summary of Data

As expected, all 150 parents were interviewed for the evaluation. Only two interviews had to be rescheduled because of unexpected conflicts. The 10 interviewers each completed 15 interviews in a 10-day period. The interviews lasted an average of 12 minutes each. A summary of the first section of the interview concerning parents' review of students' progress is presented in Table 6.1.

**Results of the Interviews**

As can be seen in Table 6.1, all but 15 of the 150 parents surveyed had talked with someone at the school about their children's progress. When asked who initiated the contact, 82 of the 135 parents said they had received a note or a telephone call from the guidance counselor regarding their child's 6-week progress report and their placement in the After School Tutorial Program. Of all the parents, 23 spoke with the homeroom teachers, who had contacted the parents. The 25 parents who talked to subject matter teachers were directly contacted by the teachers. The 12 parents who saw the assistant principal discussed students' progress in the context of pending disciplinary action. The 8 parents who saw the school's principal did so to lodge complaints.

Of the 150 parents, 110 (73%) reported grades as the topic discussed at these meetings, with need for behavior improvement identified by 42 of the parents (28%) as the second most common topic discussed with teachers. One parent could not remember exactly what had been discussed.

## Interpretation Including Pitfalls/Concerns/Cautions

The above results suggest that the high schools were successful at promoting parent involvement by reviewing student progress with parents. Of the 135 parents, 102 came to the school to review their children's progress because the guidance counselors contacted them. According to the guidance counselors' records, the five parents who did not come to school did not have telephones or had moved, and efforts to contact them through the students or by mail were unsuccessful. The five parents who had not discussed their children's progress said they would like to talk with someone at the school. This response indicates that the parents of these students were interested in the children's progress. The fact that none of the parents initiated contact with the school supports continued efforts by the high school staff to contact parents. One question to investigate concerns the possible difference

**TABLE 6.1**   Parent Contact With School Concerning Students' Progress (*n* = 150)

| *135 Parents Talked With School Personnel About Children's School Progress* | | *15 Parents Did Not Talk With School Personnel About Children's School Progress* | |
| Number | Contact | Number | Reason |
| --- | --- | --- | --- |
| 82 | Spoke with a guidance counselor | 12 | Had seen the child's most recent report card |
| 25 | Spoke with subject matter teachers | 3 | Wanted to talk with someone at school |
| 23 | Spoke with the home room teacher | | |
| 12 | Spoke with the assistant principal | | |
| 8 | Spoke with the principal | | |

between the performance of those students whose parents were successfully contacted by the high school and those who were not.

**Applying the Results**   The results of this assessment must be interpreted with caution. The sample was not necessarily representative of all parents of at-risk students in the school, and therefore drawing conclusions about the larger population from this sample should be done with care. The fact that parents were only interviewed once could have influenced the results; multiple visits might have resulted in different information.

**Reporting Results**   The evaluation team reported back to the superintendent that parent involvement was high among the parents of academically at-risk high school students. Of the total population of 300, 91% were expected to have consulted with someone at the school about their children's progress. The Afterschool Tutorial Program provided a mechanism whereby parents of at-risk students received information about students' progress.

**Evaluation Principles**   This vignette illustrated a number of important principles of good evaluation practice. These principles include the following:

1. Data collection procedures should be selected that are sensitive to the response preferences of the group being surveyed. The evaluation team selected interviews for data gathering because they thought that the parents would be more comfortable answering questions asked by an interviewer than with a paper-and-pencil task.
2. Interviews are resource intensive and usually a program does not have the personnel or time to interview everyone; some method of selecting a representative sample must be found. The evaluation team first decided to focus on the parents of students who attended the Afterschool Tutorial Program. They reasoned that this group of parents

was easily accessible and represented a large segment of the parent group of interest.

3. Interview questions and procedures need to be developed carefully, so that all the information needed, and only that information, is collected. Interviewing is so expensive that there often is no opportunity to return for a second round of questioning; all necessary information needs to be collected at one time. Further, the expense of interviewing should not be increased by asking for unnecessary information. The evaluation team carefully developed the questions and procedures for the interviews with parents. The interview protocol also was pilot tested for clarity.

4. Interviewers need to be trained so that the data collection process is uniform across interviewers. In this vignette, the interview contained a script for the interviewers to follow. The evaluation team members trained the 10 school district interviews to use the interview protocol, and interviewers received the same suggestions for presenting interviews and for writing responses to interview questions.

5. Collecting information about a program requires that the evaluators or their agents gain the trust of the people providing the information. Tutors, working at the Afterschool Tutorial Program, scheduled the interviews with parents. Parents were asked if they needed transportation, and interviews were scheduled at parents' convenience.

# Summary

This guide is intended for school personnel who want assistance with evaluating programs designed for students at risk of academic failure. Its assumes that an important purpose of evaluation is program improvement and that people who work with programs are interested in improving them. The evaluation procedures described in this guide assume some general knowledge of evaluation practices. Such general knowledge can be gained by reading *Evaluating School Programs: An Educator's Guide* (Sanders, 1992) in this series. The procedures described in this guide address a variety of program strategies, kindergarten through high school, that have been shown to be effective with at-risk students.

This guide contains suggestions for focusing an evaluation; steps to follow in the design and implementation of an evaluation; examples of how an evaluation team might evaluate a particular program component; a resource section for further reading in evaluation; a second resource section with a list of standards and indicators of program quality, including recommended evaluation methods for each indicator; and a third resource section with a reference list of evaluation reports and other sources used to identify the standards and indicators.

The six vignettes created for this guide contain a brief description of the program setting and the evaluation focus, a discussion of evaluation strategies available to the evaluation team members, a description of how information was collected using the selected strategy, a summary of the information collected, and an interpretation of how the evaluation results might be used. Each of the vignettes purposely used a different strategy for gathering information to answer evaluation questions. The strategies were selected because they represent some of the more commonly used approaches in evaluation. Only one strategy is emphasized in each of the vignettes to provide the reader with detailed information for future applications. In practice, multiple approaches and information sources are preferred.

The six vignettes presented covered the following situations and approaches: (a) assessing students' needs using focus groups, (b) identifying students for program participation and comparison groups using existing documentation, (c) determining whether or not the program improves students' attitudes toward school using existing attitude scales, (d) strengthening individualized instruction using an observation checklist, (e) verifying that school staff support the program using a written questionnaire, and (f) establishing the level of parents' involvement in the program using interviews.

# What Is in the Resources

### Resource A

Resource A provides a list of further readings in evaluation. The readings are intended to supplement the information contained in this guide. The references are not exhaustive but were selected for quality of information and clarity of style. The readings are divided into four subsections: general program evaluation approaches, selecting existing measurement instruments, constructing measurement instruments, and using qualitative/naturalistic methods. Short descriptions of these references appear in the body of this guide.

### Resource B

Resource B presents the standards and indicators of quality for the evaluation of programs for at-risk students. The standards and indicators were identified after an extensive review of programs nationwide that were successful with students at risk of academic failure. Standards express, in general terms, characteristics of high quality programs; indicators describe more specific aspects of high quality programs. School personnel generally will not use all of the standards and indicators to evaluate their program but will generally select those most important for their evaluation purposes.

### Resource C

Resource C provides the list of references used to identify the standards and indicators of quality for the evaluation of programs for at-risk students. The list contains research and evaluation reports for many different types of programs for at-risk students (e.g., early childhood enrichment programs, in-school suspension programs, and school reentry programs). School personnel, new to the field of evaluation, may use evaluation reports of similar programs to strengthen their evaluation designs.

# Resource A:
# Further Readings in Evaluation

### References for General Program Evaluation Approaches

Isaac, S., & Michael, W. B. (1985). *Handbook in research and evaluation* (2nd ed.). San Diego, CA: Edits.

Kerlinger, F. N. (1986). *Foundations of behavioral research.* New York: Holt, Rinehart & Winston.

Metfessel, N. S., & Michael, W. B. (1967). A paradigm involving multiple criterion measures for the evaluation of the effectiveness of school programs. *Educational and Psychological Measurement, 27,* 931-943.

Sanders, J. R. (1992). *Evaluating school programs: An educator's guide.* Newbury Park, CA: Corwin.

Worthen, B. R., & Sanders, J. R. (1987). *Educational evaluation: Alternative approaches and practical guidelines.* New York: Longman.

### References for Selecting Existing Measurement Instruments

Instructional Objectives Exchange. (1972). *Attitude toward school: Grades K-12.* Los Angeles: Author.

Mitchell, J. V. (1983). *Tests in print III.* Lincoln: University of Nebraska, Buros Institute of Mental Measurements.

Simon, A., & Boyer, E. G. (Eds.). (1974). *Mirrors of behavior: An anthology of observation instruments.* Philadelphia: Research for Better Schools.

### References for Constructing Measurement Instruments

Berdie, D., & Anderson, J. (1974). *Questionnaires.* Metuchen, NJ: Scarecrow.

Gallagher, J. J., Nuthall, G. A., & Rosenshine, R. (Eds.). (1970). *Classroom observation* (AERA Monograph Series in Curriculum Evaluation No. 6). Chicago: Rand McNally.

Gorden, R. L. (1975). *Interviewing: Strategy, techniques, and tactics.* Homewood, IL: Dorsey.

Henerson, M. E., Morris, L. L., & Fitz-Gibbon, C. T. (1987). *How to measure attitudes.* Newbury Park, CA: Sage.

Jaeger, R. M. (1988). Survey methods in educational research. In R. M. Jaeger (Ed.), *Complementary methods for research in education.* Washington, DC: American Educational Research Association.

McKillip, J. (1987). *Need analysis: Tools for the human services and education.* Newbury Park, CA: Sage.

## References for Using Qualitative/Naturalistic Methods

Guba, E. G., & Lincoln, Y. S. (1985). *Naturalistic inquiry.* Beverly Hills, CA: Sage.

Morgan, D. L. (1988). *Focus groups as qualitative research.* Newbury Park, CA: Sage.

Webb, E. J., Campbell, D. T., Schwartz, R. D., & Sechrest, L. (1966). *Unobtrusive measures: Non reactive research in the social sciences.* Chicago: Rand McNally.

Wolcott, H. F. (1990). *Writing up qualitative research.* Newbury Park, CA: Sage.

# Resource B:
# Standards and Indicators
# of Quality for the Evaluation
# of Programs for At-Risk Students

The standards and indicators of quality that follow in this section were initially identified as part of a project to select criteria by which to judge the quality of three programs in the Georgia public schools. One program, Special Instructional Assistance, focused on promoting language development during the early elementary grades. The second program, Remedial Education, assisted upper elementary and secondary students whose achievement had fallen behind state standards. The third program, In-School Suspension, worked with students who had classroom behavior problems.

The task of identifying standards of quality for these three programs occasioned an extensive search of the literature to identify program practices common to successful programs. Articles, programs documents, and books were consulted before arriving at the list of standards and indicators for each of those three programs for students at risk of academic failure. For the purpose of this evaluation guide, the standards and indicators for the three programs were merged, molded, and expanded to reflect high quality practices across most programs for at-risk students (kindergarten through 12th grade). A condensed bibliography from the literature consulted appears in Resource C.

The identification of standards and indicators for evaluating programs is fundamental to assessing the quality of program achievements. The standards and indicators that follow propose criteria by which the quality of programs may be judged. It is for program personnel to decide which, if any, of the standards and indicators are appropriate to the evaluation purpose(s).

## Standards and Indicators of Quality for the Evaluation of Programs for At-Risk Students

| *Standards and Indicators* | *Possible Approach* |
|---|---|

**Standard 1.** All program and school staff who work with at-risk students receive training to strengthen their ability to provide an appropriate instructional program.

| | |
|---|---|
| 1.1. All program and school staff who work with at-risk students attend in-service training sessions relevant to their work with the program during the academic year. | Existing documentation |
| 1.2. The content of in-service training sessions is based on a school's identified program needs. | Existing documentation |

**Standard 2.** The curriculum is organized in a manner that supports each student's most rapid progression toward basic-skills mastery.

| | |
|---|---|
| 2.1. Students' current basic-skills mastery levels are frequently monitored by the instructional staff. | Existing documentation |
| 2.2. Teachers keep records of students' mastery of basic skills. | Existing documentation |
| 2.3. Different content areas of the curriculum are integrated (e.g., writing is taught with science, arithmetic is taught with social studies). | Existing documentation |

**Standard 3.** Program staff employ multiple strategies to motivate students in the program.

| | |
|---|---|
| 3.1. Students are actively involved in productive activity. | Observation checklist |
| 3.2. Students are praised for success in the classroom. | Observation checklist |
| 3.3. Students are provided with assistance when needed. | Observation checklist |
| 3.4. Program staff promote students' positive attitudes toward school. | Existing attitude scale |
| 3.5. Program staff communicate their positive regard for students. | Observation checklist |
| 3.6. Program staff have high expectations for students' success. | Written questionnaire |

**Standard 4.** Instruction is individualized.

| | |
|---|---|
| 4.1. Students' assignments differ based on their assessed needs. | Existing documentation |
| 4.2. Lessons are planned to accommodate different learning style strengths and are not limited to paper-and-pencil activities. | Existing documentation |
| 4.3. Assessments of student progress include using narrative progress reports. | Existing documentation |

**Standard 5.** Instructional opportunities exist for at-risk students to interact regularly with academically successful students.

| | |
|---|---|
| 5.1. At-risk students eat lunch or participate in physical education, music, or some other activity with academically successful students as part of their school day. | Existing documentation |
| 5.2. Students engage in cooperative team learning activities with successful students. | Observation checklist<br>Existing documentation |
| 5.3. At-risk students work on group assignments with academically successful students. | Observation checklist<br>Existing documentation |

| Standards and Indicators | Possible Approach |
|---|---|
| 5.4. At-risk students receive peer tutoring from academically successful students. | Observation checklist<br>Existing documentation |
| **Standard 6.** Parents are involved in the instructional program. | |
| 6.1. Parents confer with teachers about students' progress. | Interview<br>Existing documentation |
| 6.2. Parents assist with the instructional program. | Interview<br>Existing documentation |
| 6.3. Parents attend instructional programs designed for them. | Interview<br>Existing documentation |
| **Standard 7.** Services to the students are comprehensive and well coordinated. | |
| 7.1. An individual student's progress is systematically followed, discussed, and coordinated with the parents and all key school personnel with whom the student comes in contact. | Existing documentation |
| **Standard 8.** Adequate provision is made for assessing the effectiveness of the program. | |
| 8.1. The program design is based on the needs of the group being served. | Existing documentation |
| 8.2. A comprehensive program evaluation plan is being followed and appropriate information is recorded, collected, summarized, and reported annually. | Existing documentation |
| **Standard 9.** Provision has been made for ongoing program improvement. | |
| 9.1. Program changes are implemented based on the results of the annual program evaluation. | Existing documentation |
| **Standard 10.** Students are successful in the program. | |
| 10.1. Students and their parents perceive their participation in the program as positive. | Focus group interview |
| 10.2. Students' successes are recognized in the classroom. | Observation checklist |
| 10.3. The school program staff provides leadership and support for appropriate program practices. | Written questionnaire |
| **Standard 11.** School staff actively provide the resources necessary for program success. | |
| 11.1. The school administration sees that the program is physically well equipped. | Existing documentation |
| 11.2. The school administration provides leadership and support for appropriate program practices. | Written questionnaire<br>Existing documentation |
| 11.3. Nonprogram staff in the school perceive the program as positive. | Focus group interview |

# Resource C:
# References Used to Identify
# Standards and Indicators
# of Quality
# for the Evaluation of Programs
# for At-Risk Students

Alberg, G., & Dunham, R. (1986). Keeping academically marginal youths in school: A prediction model. *Youth and Society, 17,* 346-361.

Block, E. E. (1978). *Failing students-failing schools: A study of dropouts and discipline in New York State.* New York: New York Civil Liberties Union.

Boehnlein, M. (1987). Reading intervention for high-risk first graders. *Educational Leadership, 44,* 32-37.

Bredekamp, S. (Ed.). (1987). *Developmentally appropriate practice in early childhood programs serving children from birth through age 8.* Washington, DC: National Association for the Education of Young Children.

Brophy, J. (1982). Successful teaching strategies for the inner city child. *Phi Delta Kappan, 63,* 527-530.

Burton, C. B. (1987). Children's peer relationships. In *Children's social development: Information for teachers and parents* (pp. 27-34). Urbana, IL: ERIC Clearinghouse on Elementary and Early Childhood Education.

Carbo, M., & Hodges, H. (1988). Learning styles strategies can help students at risk. *Teaching Exceptional Children, 20,* 55-58.

Chobot, R. B., & Garibaldi, A. (1982). In-school alternatives to suspension: A description of ten school district programs. *Urban Review, 14,* 317-336.

Cooke, G., & Stammer, J. (1985). Grade retention and social promotion practices. *Childhood Education, 61,* 302-308.

Cooper, G. (1979, April). Issues in cross-cultural communications. *New Directions,* pp. 18-19.

Cuddy, M. (1987). *The effects of grade retention upon the social and psychological adjustment of elementary children.* Paper presented at the annual convention of the Association for Advancement of Behavior Therapy, Boston.

Curtiss, S. (1977). *Genie: A psycholinguistic study of a modern-day "wild-child."* New York: Academic Press.

Disciullo, M. (1984). In-school suspension: An alternative to unsupervised out-of-school suspension. *The Clearing House, 57,* 328-330.

Druian, G., & Butler, J. (1987). *Effective schooling practices and at-risk youth: What the research shows.* Portland, OR: Northwest Regional Educational Laboratory. (ERIC Document Reproduction Service No. ED 291 146)

Epstein, J. L. (1988, November). *School-family-community connections to assist students at risk of failing.* Paper presented at the NMSA Pre-conference: Are We Mismatching Kids and Schools? Denver, CO.

Evans, R. (1984). Children with special needs in the ordinary school: An approach to intervention using "remedial" teachers in a preventive role. *Early Child Development and Care, 18,* 61-104.

Garber, H., Sunshine, P., & Reed, C. (1989, March). *Collaborative study on dropout reduction of at-risk youth: A preliminary analysis.* Paper presented at the annual meeting of the American Educational Research Association, San Francisco.

Georgia Department of Education. (1988). *Public school standards.* Atlanta: Georgia Public Schools.

Georgia Department of Education. (1989). *Guidelines for special instructional assistance.* Atlanta: Georgia Public Schools.

Glass, G. V., & Smith, M. L. (1979). Meta-analysis of the research on class size and achievement. *Educational Evaluation and Policy Analysis, 1,* 2-16.

Glatthorn, A. A. (1985, May). *Curriculum reform and "at-risk" youth.* Paper presented at the Research for Better Schools, Inc., Conference, Philadelphia.

Grice, M. (1986). *Positive alternatives to school suspension.* Portland, OR: Portland Public Schools. (ERIC Document Reproduction Service No. ED 276 794)

Hamby, J. V. (1989). How to get an "A" on your dropout prevention report card. *Educational Leadership, 46,* 21-28.

Hamilton, S. F. (1986). Raising standards and reducing dropout rates. *Teachers College Record, 87,* 410-429.

Hess, G. A., & Lauber, D. (1985). *Dropouts from the Chicago Public Schools: An analysis of the classes of 1982, 1983, 1984.* Chicago: Chicago Panel on Public School Finance. (ERIC Document Reproduction Service No. ED 258 095)

Higgins, C. (1988). *Youth motivation: At-risk youth talk to program planners.* Philadelphia: Public/Private Ventures. (ERIC Document Reproduction Service No. ED 300 486)

Hochman, S., & Worner, W. (1987). In-school suspension and group counseling: Helping the at-risk student. *NASSP Bulletin, 71*(501), 93-96.

Hollifield, J. H. (Ed.). (1989). *Success for all.* Washington, DC: Johns Hopkins University, CREMS.

Holmes, C. (1983). The fourth R: Retention. *Journal of Research and Development in Education, 17,* 1-6.

Holmes, C. (1986). *A synthesis of recent research on nonpromotion: A five year follow-up.* Paper presented at the annual meeting of the American Educational Research Association, San Francisco.

Isenhart, L., & Bechard, S. (1987). *Dropout prevention: The Education Commission of the States' survey of state initiatives for youth at risk.* Denver, CO: Education Commission of the States.

Jennings, G. (1987). Half-steps from kindergarten to second grade. Special report: Early childhood education. *Principal, 66,* 22-24.

Johnson, D. W., & Johnson, R. T. (1986). Mainstreaming and cooperative learning strategies. *Exceptional Children, 52,* 553-561.

Katz, L., & Chard, S. (1988). *Engaging the minds of young children: The project approach.* Norwood, NJ: Ablex.

Lehr, J. B., & Harris, H. W. (1988). *At risk, low-achieving students in the classroom* (Analysis and action series). Washington, DC: National Education Association. (ERIC Document Reproduction Service No. ED 298 232)

Leitner, D. (1989, March). *"Effective school practices" in compensatory education programs.* Paper presented at the annual meeting of the American Educational Research Association, San Francisco.

Levin, H. M. (1987). Accelerated school for disadvantaged students. *Educational Leadership, 44,* 19-21.

Levin, H. M. (1989). Financing the education of at-risk students. *Educational Evaluation and Policy Analysis, 11,* 47-60.

Levin, H. M., Glass, G. V., & Meister, G. R. (1987). A cost-effectiveness analysis of computer assisted instruction. *Evaluation Review, 11,* 50-72.

Lloyd, D. N. (1978). Prediction of school failure from third-grade data. *Educational and Psychological Measurement, 38,* 1193-1200.

Madden, N. A., & Slavin, R. E. (1987, April). *Effective pull-out programs for students at risk.* Paper presented at the annual meeting of the American Educational Research Association, Washington, DC.

Madden, N. A., Slavin, R. E., Karweit, N. L., & Livermon, B. J. (1989). Success for all: Restructuring the urban elementary school. *Educational Leadership, 46,* 14-18.

Miller, D. (1986). Effect of a program of therapeutic discipline on the attitude, attendance, and insight of truant adolescents. *Journal of Experimental Education, 55,* 49-53.

Montgomery County Public Schools. (1981). *A preliminary evaluation of the Pilot In-School Suspension Program, 1980-81.* Rockville, MD: Department of Educational Accountability.

Moresi, M., & Lovelace, T. (1986). *Evaluation report: State-funded compensatory/remedial program, 1985-86 academic year.* Lafayette, LA: Lafayette Parish School Board. (ERIC Document Reproduction Service No. ED 300 437)

National Diffusion Network. (1989). *Educational programs that work* (15th ed.). Longmont, CO: Sopris West.

Niklason, L. (1984). Nonpromotion: A pseudoscientific solution. *Psychology in the Schools, 21,* 485-499.

O'Sullivan, R. G., & Tennant, C. V. (1989). *Draft standards and indicators for evaluation of In-School Suspension programs in Georgia's public schools.* Greensboro, NC: Center for Educational Research and Evaluation.

Piaget, J. (1952). *The child's conception of number*. London: Routledge & Kegan Paul.

Rawers, L. J. (1983). *Precision teaching: Advancing student achievement through daily drill and measurement*. Eugene: Oregon School Study Council. (ERIC Document Reproduction Service No. ED 238 184)

Rist, R. C. (1973). *The urban school a factory for failure: A study of education in American society*. Cambridge: MIT Press.

Rumberger, R. W. (1987). High school dropouts: A review of issues and evidence. *Review of Educational Research, 57*, 101-121.

Rutter, R. A. (1988, April). *Effects of school as a community*. Paper presented at the annual meeting of the American Educational Research Association, New Orleans, LA.

Schachter, F. F., & Strage, A. A. (1982). Adults' talk and children's language development. In S. G. Moore & C. R. Cooper (Eds.), *The young child: Reviews of research* (Vol. 3, pp. 79-96). Washington, DC: NAEYC.

Shepard, L., & Smith, M. (1987). Effects of kindergarten retention at the end of first grade. *Psychology in the Schools, 24*, 346-357.

Slavin, R. E. (1980). Cooperative learning. *Review of Educational Research, 50*, 315-342.

Slavin, R. E., & Madden, N. A. (1987). *Effective classroom programs for students at risk*. Paper presented at the annual meeting of the American Educational Research Association, Washington, DC.

Slavin, R. E., & Madden, N. A. (1989). What works for students at risk: A research synthesis. *Educational Leadership, 46*, 4-13.

Stern, D. (1986). *Dropout prevention and recovery in California*. Unpublished paper, University of California, Berkeley.

Syropoulos, M. (1987). *High school development center: An alternative school for ninth and tenth grades*. Detroit, MI: Detroit Public Schools, Department of Evaluation and Testing. (ERIC Document Reproduction Service No. ED 298 227)

U.S. General Accounting Office. (1987). *School dropouts: Survey of local programs* (Report to congressional requesters; GAO/HRD-87-108 School Dropout Programs). Washington, DC: Author.

Walker, N. (1984). Elementary school grade retention: Avoiding abuses through systematic decision-making. *Journal of Research and Development in Education, 18*, 1-6.

Yukish, J. (1988). Reading recovery: Early help for at-risk readers. *Updating-School-Board-Policies, 19*, 1-3.

# Index